MORE Faith-Building with Preschoolers

Teachers and Parents Together

Linda Prenzlow and Ilene Allinger Candreva

Illustrated by Becky Radtke

CPH
SAINT LOUIS

Scripture quotations taken from the HOLY BIBLE, NEW INTERNATIONAL VERSION®. NIV®. Copyright © 1973, 1978, 1984 by International Bible Society. Used by permission of Zondervan Publishing House. All rights reserved.

Copyright © 1999 Concordia Publishing House
3558 S. Jefferson Avenue, St. Louis, MO 63118-3968
Manufactured in the United States of America

1   2   3   4   5   6   7   8   9   10   08   07   06   05   04   03   02   01   00   99

To the Lord, who has blessed me so greatly. To my parents, who laid the foundation of my faith. To Gee and Alex, my precious gifts from God.—Linda

To SBC & TBS & Tara—promises kept. And, of course, to Phil, Kip, and Andy.
—Ilene

Contents

Introduction

How to Use This Book

It is both a blessing and a challenge to teach children the developmental skills of sharing, following directions, using words, helping, listening, and telling the truth. God is our first teacher and ultimate guide in the task of learning and practicing these skills. This book uses Bible memory verses, child development information, Bible characters/ stories, classroom activities, and family-centered projects to teach preschoolers these six basic developmental skills. Activities are designed to address the social, emotional, intellectual, and physical tasks of a preschooler's development.

Each unit will provide ample time for repetition, repetition, and more repetition—the best way for preschoolers to absorb and understand the teaching objectives. Through the **Parent's Letter** and **Family Activities**, classroom lessons will be reinforced at home and children will learn that God's Word is an integral part of their daily lives.

Bible Memory Verse

- **The foundation**. The teaching objective is based on God's Word.

- **Memorize the verse**. If you want the children to value learning this verse, they must see that you have memorized it for your own personal growth. Help your students memorize it through repetition and application.

Teacher's Prayer

- **Copy it** and put it on your desk.

- **Pray it** as you start each day and prepare to teach.

- **Reflect on it**. Gain strength for your task, guidance for modeling God's Word and the teaching objective, and share the joy of your accomplishments with God.

Teaching Objective

- **Identify the developmental skill and Bible character introduced by each unit.**

- **Set your teaching goal and evaluate the children's learning.**

How Children Learn

- **Establish learning expectations** for each child and for your class as a whole.

- **Alter activities and expectations.** Adjust for the children's developmental level. 3-year-olds have very short attention spans; expect to plan many activities for each day. 5-year-olds can focus on a task and have greater interest in creating a product—activities will probably last longer.

- **Activities might not work out as you had planned.** Read this section again and try to adjust your expectations or the activities for a better fit with the developmental levels.

- **Each child develops differently.** Do not force a child to do art projects or participate in Circle Time if she is not yet interested. Respect each child's God-given abilities and interests.

- **Preschoolers learn best by doing.** In each of these units, the story is placed *after* the activities. Preschoolers don't have a lot of life experience, so they learn better by doing activities that build upon each other and then tying it all together with a Bible story. The activities become the foundation for the learning. The children will listen and understand more if the story starts to make sense for them. A 3-year-old has no understanding of Jesus as the Good Shepherd if he has never seen a sheep and has no idea what a shepherd does to take care of his sheep. If you first show the child the sheep, compare it to animals he already knows, and talk about what it means to care for sheep, the child will be able to make connections when the class learns the concept of Jesus as the Good Shepherd.

- **Teach the units in a way that works best for your class.** Feel free to adapt activities, stories, or the order of the unit for your individual class or classes. The key is to help preschoolers understand and apply the concepts of patience, kindness and gentleness, friendship, forgiveness, thankfulness, and courage.

Teaching Activities

Decorate the Bible Memory Verse

- **Prepare for the mess.** Most of the Bible memory verses are independent art projects requiring a minimum of adult assistance. Set up the art projects to minimize the mess; use newspapers, shower curtains, or other coverings for work surfaces and floors.

- **Emphasize process, not product.** Resist the urge to make the pictures "look pretty." Comment on the child's use of color and texture, willingness to try, and feelings during the experience, rather than on the finished product.

- **Encourage appropriate use of art materials.** Show the children how to use the art materials correctly. After giving instructions, let the children enjoy using the paint, glue, scissors, pencils, or other art materials with a minimum of direction. Try to distinguish between a child's inability to use a material and inappropriate use of the material, and provide guidance accordingly. Encourage exploration.

- **Recite the verse.** Ask the children to repeat the verse. Help them memorize the verse, including its reference (book, chapter, and verse).

- **Connect the story.** Help the children retell the Bible story. Prompt when necessary, ask questions, and correct major errors. Make sure the children can identify each unit's teaching objective.

- **Send it home.** Encourage students to display the decorated Bible Memory Verse in their kitchen, bedroom, or bathroom, wherever they are most likely to see and practice the verse. You might also want to keep some projects in the classroom on a bulletin board display during the month.

Keeping the Teaching Objective Alive in the Classroom

- **Invest the time.** These projects require some extra work on your part, but they will provide many opportunities for your children to learn and practice each unit's teaching objective in their daily life. These ideas provide continuity for the teaching objective and serve as a focal point for the Bible memory verse, Bible story, and activities.

- **Repeat the unit's teaching objective.** When your children are using this activity, repeat the unit teaching objective often: "be patient," "be kind and gentle," "be a friend," "say I'm sorry," "say thank you," and "be brave."

Circle Time Ideas

- **Motion reinforces learning.** Children remember 90 percent of what they do and only 10 percent of what they hear. These activities provide an opportunity to act out the Bible stories, Bible memory verses, and teaching objectives, making the children more likely to incorporate the objectives into their daily lives.

- **Repeat the teaching objective.** Repeat the Bible memory verse and teaching objective often during this activity.

- **Use them more than once.** Repetition increases learning.

Art and Craft Projects

- **Prepare for the mess.**
- **Emphasize process rather than product.**
- **Encourage appropriate use of the art materials.**

Other Activities

- **Use the activities often.**
- **Vary the activities.**
- **Repeat popular activities.** Favorite activities from a unit can be repeated in following units. Find ways to incorporate each unit's teaching objective with activities from previous units. Use these repeated activities as a way of reviewing previous units.

Telling the Story

- **Rehearse the story.** Plan hand gestures, voice changes, eye contact, and other movements you can use when telling the story. Tell the story with enthusiasm and excitement. This is God's Word!

- **Assemble all the props.** Practice with the props. Be comfortable with them. They should add to the spoken story, not detract from it.

- **Repeat the unit's teaching objective often.** Preschoolers learn best through repetition.

Parent's Letter & Family Activities

- **Fill in the blanks.** For example, include deadline dates for contributions to the classroom.

- **Sign the letter.**

- **Tell the children what's in the letter.** Stimulate their curiosity about the activities and encourage them to ask their parents to read the letter and try the Family Activities.

- **Send it home.** As simple as this sounds, parents cannot be partners in teaching if they do not know what's happening in the classroom. They need the information and activities contained in this letter to reinforce the teaching objectives at home.

- **Follow up.** Ask the children if they have done any of the activities with their families. Encourage them to share their experiences. When you meet a child's parents, tell them that you value them as partners with you in their child's education. Inspire them to try some of the activities described in each unit and praise them when they join you in the blessed challenge of teaching developmental skills through God's Word.

Be Patient!

Abraham and Sarah Wait for a Son

Bible Memory Verse

Be still before the LORD and wait patiently for Him. *Psalm 37:7*

Teacher's Prayer

Heavenly Father, it is so hard to wait. I want the children to learn the classroom rules, the alphabet and numbers, and how to get along with others, RIGHT NOW. Help me remember Abraham and Sarah's patience as they waited for Your promised gift of a son. Help me show patience with my students so they will learn to be patient also. In Jesus' name I pray. Amen.

Teaching Objective: Patience

To help children learn patience, just as Abraham and Sarah waited patiently for their son, Isaac.

Through God's Word and the power of the Holy Spirit, by the end of this unit, the children should be able to:

1. Tell the basic story of Abraham and Sarah.

2. Repeat the Bible memory verse.

3. Comprehend the teaching objective *patience*.

4. Show an increased ability to be patient.

5. Demonstrate the difference between gentle and rough touch, action, and behavior toward others.

Learning patience takes time and practice. In order to be patient, children must understand time, trust that their patience will be rewarded, and learn how to occupy themselves while they are waiting. You can help the children learn to be patient by recognizing and remembering how children are patient at different ages and developmental stages.

How Children Learn to Be Patient

Age 3: 3-year-olds are impatient and still in the beginning stages of learning self-control.

A 3-year-old can learn much about patience by experiencing a calm and patient environment. At 3, a rush, rush, "hurry-up" atmosphere intensifies the already movement-oriented, short-attention-span, "I-want-it-now" approach to life. Being patient with a dawdler and displaying a calm attitude in the classroom sets the stage for experiencing patience. A 3-year-old child understands concrete examples. Rather than saying, "Be patient," say, "We'll have a snack when everyone is sitting quietly at the table." Or, "I'll get the ball for you when I finish tying Sara's shoe." If required to wait a long time, a 3-year-old will wait more patiently if she is distracted or guided into activities that take the focus off "waiting." Singing songs while waiting in line makes the wait more manageable.

Age 4: 4-year-olds are learning to direct their own activities. Tell a 4-year-old, "We will have story time when the big hand is straight up on the clock. You can help pick up the blocks while you are waiting." You can be a good model of patience and self-distraction; instead of watching your class while they work on a project, step off to the side and calmly sort puzzle pieces, rearrange reading corner books, or organize art supplies. Help a 4-year-old through a frustrating task by breaking it into steps, praising him for problem solving, and encouraging him to try again later if he decides to quit.

Age 5: A 5-year-old can better practice patience when told how long to wait and why. Her understanding of time and comparisons is expanding. You can tell a 5-year-old, "The bus will arrive in half an hour. That's how long Mister Rogers' Neighborhood lasts." "We can't have recess now because the grade-schoolers are using the playground. It will be our turn after story time." You can help children increase their patience by designing projects or activities with delayed rewards. Planting a classroom garden or earning points toward a reward for reading books are activities that teach patience, perseverance, and delayed gratification.

Teaching Activities

Decorating the Bible Memory Verse: Patience Prints

Materials Needed

- Copy of the Bible memory verse (page 13)
- Bright-colored copy paper, one per child
- Copies of Isaac's Baby Things (page 14)
- Scissors
- Clear tape
- A sunny day

What to Do

1. Photocopy the Bible memory verse on to bright-colored copy paper, one per child. Bright colors work better than pastels and dark colors work better than light ones.
2. Make enough copies of Isaac's Baby Things so each child will have 4 or 5 objects.
3. Cut out the baby things.
4. Place the memory verses, the baby things, and the tape on your art table.

Continue to set up for this art project as normal.

5. Show the children how to make loops of tape to use to tape the baby things onto their Bible memory verses.
6. Place each Bible memory verse in direct sunlight for several hours; a full day is best.
7. Help the children carefully remove the baby things. Note how the paper has faded and left the outline of the baby things.

Teaching Patience

- Name the baby things for the children. Be sure to tell them that Isaac, born four thousand years ago, would have had different baby things than the familiar items in the pictures.
- Making tape loops can be hard work for little hands. Praise the children as they patiently try to make them. Encourage those who get frustrated; reassure them that they will eventually be able to make them. They just have to wait and grow up a little more!
- Waiting and waiting and waiting for the project to be done is tedious for youngsters. Praise the children as they wait. Help them repeat the story, recalling how Abraham and Sarah waited patiently for their son, Isaac.
- Read the Bible memory verse individually with the children. Help them list times they have had to wait patiently.

Keeping the Teaching Objective Alive in the Classroom—Patient Plants

Materials Needed

- An old wagon (metal is best)
- A hand drill

- Gravel
- Potting soil
- Seeds such as lettuce, cucumber, water-melon, zinnia, and marigold
- Watering can

  OR

- Eggshell halves, one per child
- Egg cartons, enough to hold the shells
- Potting soil
- 3–5 small cups
- 6–10 spoons
- Eyedropper

What to Do

1. If using the wagon, use the hand drill to drill about 7–10 holes in the bottom of the wagon. This will allow excess water to drain.

2. Place a layer of gravel in the bottom of the wagon, then fill the wagon with potting soil.

3. Help the children sprinkle the seeds onto the dirt. Cover the seeds with a thin layer of soil.

4. Water your garden.

5. Wheel the garden into the sun daily. Be sure to rotate the task of watering the garden among the children.

   OR

1. Carefully wash the eggshells.

2. Before school starts, set up for this project as you would for any assisted, messy project. Place the potting soil into small cups. Put two spoons in each cup.

3. Help the children patiently spoon the potting soil into their eggshells. Gently tap it down.

4. Sprinkle the seeds onto the dirt and cover them with a thin layer of soil.

5. Have the children use the eye dropper to water their eggshell.

Teaching Patience

- Waiting for seeds to sprout requires patience. Help the children keep track of the number of days they wait. Praise them for each new day of patience.

- Sarah had to wait years and years to get pregnant and then nine more months to have Isaac. As your children impatiently examine the dirt for some sign of life, speculate with them how Sarah might have felt. When the seeds sprout, ask the children how they think she felt when Isaac was finally born.

- The children still must wait for the new sprouts to mature and bloom or bear vegetables. Ask the children how this waiting reminds them of the story. Is it like when Sarah was waiting for Isaac to grow up?

Waiting to Move: A Circle-Time Game to Teach Patience

Materials Needed

- A source of music: radio, CD player, or tape player.

What to Do

1. Set up the music.

2. During Circle Time, explain to the children that they dance when the music is played and freeze when the music stops. Encourage them to remain frozen until the music starts again, then remind them to dance again.

Teaching Patience

- This game develops listening skills and

encourages following directions. Praise the children who successfully listen and carefully follow the rules.

- It might be difficult for some children to freeze, especially the "wiggly" ones. At some time during the game, make a point to praise each child for patiently waiting to dance.

- Ask the children if they think Sarah did a dance when she found out she was pregnant. Who else might have danced in the story? Who had to wait patiently?

Painting a Picture: An Art Project to Teach Patience

Materials Needed

- Rubber cement
- Fingerpaint paper, at least one piece for each child
- Watercolor paints
- Brushes

What to Do

1. On the first day, put the paper and rubber cement on the art table. Help the children drip rubber cement onto their paper. Let it dry overnight.

2. On the second day, put the rubber cement dribbled papers on the art table. Show the children how to paint the entire paper with the water colors. Let them dry overnight.

3. On the third day, help the children peel away the rubber cement to discover a design.

Teaching Patience

- This project, because of its long drying time, demands patience. Help the children wait by offering praise and encouragement.

- Each step is exciting and fun, in and of itself. The end product, however, is worth the wait. Compare this to the Bible story: each step (entertaining the angels, being pregnant, holding the baby) was also exciting for the prospective parents. However, Isaac as the end result, was definitely a miracle—well worth the wait.

Isaac's Here: A Center Activity to Teach the Story

Materials Needed

- Dolls
- Doll clothes
- Cradle or crib
- Blankets
- Baby feeding supplies: bottle, spoon, food, etc.

What to Do

1. Set up this center activity as normal.

2. Encourage all the children to practice taking care of the babies. Show them how to hold, rock, nurture, and feed them.

Teaching Patience

- Remind the children that Sarah would have been very attentive to Isaac's needs because she had waited so many years for a baby.

- Babies require patience, lots of patience. Help the children act out successful resolutions to difficult, patience-trying situations such as a baby who is crying, hungry, or sleepy. Praise them for their persistence and patience in difficult times.

- Encourage the children to use the babies to act out the story of Abraham, Sarah, and Isaac. While they may not remember all the details, be sure they have a general understanding of the story. Help them repeat the unit's teaching objective: Be patient!

First Things First: A Center Activity to Teach Patience

Materials Needed

- Sequence Cards (pages 15–17)
- Scissors
- 3 sheets of heavy white paper
- Glue
- Markers, one color for each Sequence Set
- A small basket (berry baskets work well)

What to Do

1. Make copies of the Sequence Cards (pages 15–17).

2. Glue all the Sequence Cards to the heavy white paper.

3. Turn the cards over. Number the cards on the back of each Sequence card. Place a number 1 on the first card of the set, a number 2 on the second, and so on. Use a different color marker for each set.

4. When the glue is dry, cut along the dotted lines.

5. Put the Sequence Cards in the small basket. If your class is primarily younger children, separate each set of cards. Paper clip them together or use a different berry basket for each set. Color code the basket to match the colors of the numbers.

6. Introduce this activity as you would any new learning center. Show the children how to put the cards in the correct order.

7. When the children have finished sequencing, show them how to self-check the work by using the colored numbers on the back of the Sequence Cards.

Teaching Patience

- This activity requires children to sit still and persevere. Praise them for working patiently, just like Abraham and Sarah.

- Encourage the children to tell you about times they have waited similar to those pictured on the Sequence Cards.

- Remember, preschoolers love repetition. If appropriate, repeat any of the praises or suggestions for teaching patience described elsewhere in this unit.

Patient Pairs: A Circle-Time Game to Teach the Bible Memory Verse

Materials Needed

- Copy of the Bible memory verse (page 13)

What to Do

1. During Circle Time, repeat the Bible memory verse several times with the children.

2. Divide the group into pairs. Assign one person in each pair to be the "mover," the other person to be the "waiter." Assure the students that they will each switch roles.

3. The mover has three jobs: to move when the Bible memory verse is being spoken, to freeze when the Bible memory verse ends, and to move the tiniest body part slowly. The waiter has two jobs: to say the Bible memory verse and to spot the body part the mover is moving.

4. Say the verse aloud with the waiters while the movers dance. Help the waiters spot the tiniest body part that the mover is moving. Switch roles and repeat. Do this several times.

Teaching Patience

- It is hard to freeze. Praise the movers when they are able to be patient enough to freeze.

- Spotting a tiny change or movement can be difficult too. Encourage your waiters to persevere and to search for the movement. Rejoice with them when they find it.

Waiting for the Wind: A Craft Project to Teach the Bible Memory Verse

Materials Needed

- Clean frozen juice cans, one per child
- 18" crepe paper streamers, 4 per child
- 12" piece of yarn, one per child
- Glue
- Tape
- Staplers
- Scissors, child-sized
- Crayons
- Copies of the Wind Sock memory verse (page 18), one per child

What to Do

1. Remove both the top and bottom lids of the juice cans. Be sure the cans are clean and dry.

2. Follow your normal procedure for setting up the art table.

3. Help the children cut out the Wind Sock memory verse by cutting on the solid lines. Help them decorate it with the crayons. Show them how to glue the verse around the juice cans.

4. Help the children tape the crepe paper streamers on one end of the can.

5. Show them how to staple both ends of the yarn to the can, making a handle.

Teaching Patience

- Cutting along the lines, taping crepe paper streamers, and stapling handles can be tedious work for little hands. Encourage the children to be patient and to finish the project. It is the creative process, more than the finished product, that will help the children learn patience.

- Read the Bible memory verse individually with the children. Help them recall times they have had to wait upon the Lord to do something—or to wait upon their parents! Guide them in recalling the main points of the Bible story.

- Hang the wind sock outside and encourage the children to wait patiently for the Lord to send wind to blow it. Talk about how difficult it is to wait. Remind the children that Sarah and Abraham probably had a hard time waiting for baby Isaac to be born.

Telling the Story

Before telling the story, refresh your memory by reading Genesis 12:1–8 and 21:1–5. To tell the story, you will need five adult dolls (four males, one female) from your class's doll house; an empty file folder; some doll-size dishes (4 plates, 1 bucket); an empty cradle; and a baby doll. Hand out the props, except for the file folder, to the children. Instruct them to wait patiently for their turn to use them as you tell the story. Fold down three inches on each long side of the file folder. Set the file folder in front of you to use as Abraham's tent. Read the story (bold print) and follow the instructions (italic print).

Raise your hand if you were ever a baby. Is everyone raising their hands? Yes, every one of you was once a baby. How many of you have a younger brother or sister at home? Do you remember waiting for your brother or sister to be born? How long did you wait? *Pause for answers.* **Well, here's a true story from the Bible about a man and a woman who waited almost 100 years for a baby.**

One day, Abraham was sitting at the door of his tent, waiting patiently for the hot part of the day to be over. *Sit the Abraham doll in front of the tent.* **He looked up and saw three men.** *Have the children with the other three dolls hold them in a group, standing close to Abraham.* **When Abraham saw them, he hurried out to meet them. He did not want them to stand outside in the hot sun.** *Help the Abraham doll run out to meet the three dolls.* **Abraham did not know it, but the three men were really angels from the Lord. Abraham said to them, "Please do not continue your journey in this hot time of the day; please stop and wait for the cool of the evening. I will bring you some water to wash your feet, and something to eat. Then you can rest for a while before you go on your way."**

"All right," said the three angels. "We will stay here until it is cool enough to travel." *Sit the three angel dolls in front of the tent. Have the child holding the Sarah doll place it in the tent. Put the Abraham doll inside the tent.*

Abraham hurried into the tent to his wife, Sarah. "Quick," he said, "bake some bread and cook some meat." Then Abraham hurried back to the three angels with some water so they could wash their feet. *Have Abraham exit the tent carrying the miniature bucket. Give the bucket to the three angel dolls.* **When everything was ready, Abraham served dinner to his three patient guests.** *Help the Abraham doll to carry the miniature plates out to his guests.*

"Where is your wife, Sarah?" one of the angels asked him. "There, in the tent," Abraham said. Then the angel said, "I will come back to see you next year, and Sarah, your wife, will have a son."

Inside the tent, Sarah was listening to the men talk. When she heard the visitors promise her a baby, she started to laugh. Sarah thought, "I am 90 years old. Abraham is 100 years old. We have waited and waited and waited for a baby. Will I really have a child? I don't think so!" *Set the empty cradle in the middle of the circle.*

Then the angel said, "Why did Sarah laugh and say, 'Will I really have a child?' Does she think a baby is too hard for the Lord? I will return to you next year and Sarah will have a son." Then the angels left. *Remove the three angel dolls.*

Sarah and Abraham waited for their son. They waited and waited and waited. Then they waited some more. *Rock the empty cradle.* **Finally, Sarah became pregnant and gave birth to a son, at the very time God had promised.**

Abraham named the baby Isaac, which means laughter. Abraham held a great feast to celebrate Isaac's birth. Abraham and Sarah had waited patiently; God answered their patience with a wonderful son. *Place the baby doll in the cradle.*

Bible Memory Verse

Be still before the LORD and wait patiently for Him.

Psalm 37:7 (NIV)

Isaac's Baby Things

Sequence Cards

Sequence Cards

Sequence Cards

Wind Sock Bible Memory Verse

Be still before the LORD and wait patiently for Him.

Psalm 37:7 (NIV)

Be still before the LORD and wait patiently for Him.

Psalm 37:7 (NIV)

Be still before the LORD and wait patiently for Him.

Psalm 37:7 (NIV)

Be still before the LORD and wait patiently for Him.

Psalm 37:7 (NIV)

Dear Parent(s),

"Be patient!" As a parent, you instruct, beg, demand, and sometimes even whine these words to your child. Preschoolers must learn patience in order to successfully complete projects, make commitments, solve problems, and develop positive relationships.

This month, our class will learn about Abraham and Sarah and their long, patient wait for a baby. The lessons of Abraham and Sarah and patience shouldn't stop at the classroom door. I invite you to share these lessons with your child at home by reading the story of Abraham and Sarah from a preschool Bible, trying the activities provided in this letter, and teaching this Bible memory verse.

Be still before the LORD and wait patiently for Him. *Psalm 37:7*

How Children Learn to Be Patient

Age 3: 3-year-olds are impatient and still in the beginning stages of learning self-control.

A 3-year-old can learn much about patience by experiencing a calm and patient environment. At 3, a rush, rush, "hurry-up" atmosphere intensifies the already movement-oriented, short-attention-span, "I-want-it-now" approach to life. Being patient with a dawdler and displaying a calm attitude in the home sets the stage for experiencing patience. A 3-year-old child understands concrete examples. Rather than saying, "Be patient," say, "We'll have a snack when everyone is sitting quietly at the table." Or, "I'll get the ball for you when I finish tying Sara's shoe." If required to wait a long time, a 3-year-old will wait more patiently if she is distracted or guided into activities that take the focus off "waiting." Singing songs while waiting in line makes the wait more manageable.

Age 4: 4-year-olds are learning to direct their own activities. Tell a 4-year-old, "We will read a book when the big hand is straight up on the clock. You can help pick up the blocks while you are waiting." You can be a good model of patience and self-distraction; instead of watching your child work on a task, step off to the side and calmly sort puzzle pieces, rearrange toys, or organize supplies. Help a 4-year-old through a frustrating task by breaking it into steps, praising him for problem solving, and encouraging him to try again later if he decides to quit.

Age 5: A 5-year-old can better practice patience when told how long to wait and why. Her understanding of time and comparisons is expanding. You can tell a 5-year-old, "The bus will arrive in half an hour. That's how long Mister Rogers' Neighborhood lasts." You can help children increase their patience by designing projects or activities with delayed rewards. Planting a garden or earning points toward a reward for reading books are activities that teach patience, perseverance, and delayed gratification.

Learning to be patient takes time and practice. In order to be patient, children must understand time, trust that their patience will be rewarded, and learn how to occupy themselves while they are waiting. You can help teach your child patience by understanding how children learn patience at different ages.

Parents must practice patience even more than their children. As you struggle to be patient with your child, control your temper, and maintain a calm and peaceful life, turn to your heavenly Father in prayer.

Parent's Prayer

Heavenly Father, it is so hard to wait. I want my child to learn our household rules, the alphabet and numbers, and how to get along with others RIGHT NOW. Help me remember Abraham and Sarah's patience as they waited for Your promised gift of a son. Help me show patience so my child might learn to be patient also. In Jesus' name I pray. Amen.

Together in Christ,

Family Activities

Frozen Fruit Treats: A Cooking Adventure

Ingredients

1 cup vanilla yogurt

1 banana, sliced

or, 1 cup of your child's favorite fruit, sliced into bite-sized pieces

1 cup fruit juice

What to Do

1. Help your child pour all the ingredients into a blender. Cover it and let the child push the button to make the blender whirl. Continue blending until the ingredients are thoroughly mixed.

2. Pour the mixture into small cups. Help your child stand a plastic spoon or craft stick in each cup.

3. Place the cups in the freezer.

4. When frozen, eat!

Teaching Patience

- Is your child having a hard time waiting for this sweet treat? Together, come up with a list of constructive ways to fill the time until the frozen treats are ready. Then do some of the things on that list together!

- Compliment any signs of patience your child exhibits when waiting for the sweet treats. Patience, after all, is built slowly. Your child has to start somewhere!

- Tell your child that Abraham and Sarah might have eaten the basic ingredients for this treat: yogurt, fresh fruit, and juice. They did not, however, have the technology to freeze the mixture into frozen treats. Isn't your child glad to be living now and to enjoy these sweets?

- Help your child repeat the story of Isaac's birth by asking these questions: Who prepared the food in the story? (Abraham) Who were his guests? (Three angels in disguise) What did Abraham and Sarah learn after their meal? (Sarah would have a baby.)

Waiting for Forever: A Craft Project

Materials Needed

- Wide-mouthed jar
- Water
- Borax, about 3 tablespoons per cup of water
- Food coloring
- Pipe cleaners
- String
- Pencil

What to Do

1. Help your child bend a pipe cleaner into the infinity symbol. ∞

2. Tie one end of the string around the center of the infinity symbol. Tie the other end around the pencil. If your child can tie knots, you might want to let her try this step.

3. Fill the jar with boiling water.

4. Mix the borax into the heated water, about one tablespoon at a time. Help your child stir in more borax until the powder settles on the bottom of the jar.

5. If you like, stir in a single color of food coloring.

6. Rest the pencil across the top of the jar so the infinity symbol is suspended in the borax and water solution. Be sure the symbol does not touch the bottom of the jar; you might need to adjust the length of the string.

7. Set the jar aside overnight. By morning, the symbol should be covered with glittery crystals, made from the borax clumping together.

8. Remove the symbol from the jar. Let it drip-dry over the sink.

Teaching Patience

- Tying knots is hard for most children. Encourage your child to try this task, but do not expect it to be mastered until age 6 or so. Perseverance in a difficult task helps build patience.

- Explain to your child what the infinity symbol means: forever or without number. Ask how that symbol is like God; be prepared for some unconventional answers. Guide your child into understanding that God goes on forever, and there is no limit to His love.

- Waiting overnight to see the finished product can be difficult. Praise your child during the struggle to wait.

Building a House: A Trip to Take

Materials Needed

- A building site you drive past regularly

What to Do

1. Make repeated visits to the building site.
2. Keep track of the number of days it takes the workers to complete the task.
3. Rejoice when the building is complete!

Teaching Patience

- Talk about what the structure might become: a store, a mall, a house. Speculate on who might live there or how it might be used. Guess how many days it will take to finish the project. When the building is completed, see who was closest.

- Compliment your child for waiting patiently as the structure is completed. As you drive to and from the building site, help your child repeat the story of Abraham and Sarah.

Other Simple Ideas

1. As you wait in line or at a red light, tell your child, "I am waiting patiently for the light to change to green so we can go."
2. Make up a "waiting song" to sing during short waiting times.
3. Pack a "waiting bag" to take to restaurants, doctor appointments, etc. Include crayons, notebooks, small toys, a storybook, and a simple snack.

Be Kind and Gentle!

Ruth Takes Care of Naomi

Bible Memory Verse

Be kind ... to one another. *Ephesians 4:32*

Teacher's Prayer

Heavenly Father, Ruth was kind and showed Your love as she cared for Naomi. Help me to model the same kind, helpful love for my students so they may understand Your love and, in turn, offer it to others. In Jesus' name I pray. Amen.

Teaching Objective: Kindness & Gentleness

To help children learn to be kind and gentle, just as Ruth was kind to Naomi and took care of her.

Through God's Word and the power of the Holy Spirit, by the end of this unit, the children should be able to:

1. Tell the basic story of Ruth and Naomi.

2. Repeat the Bible memory verse.

3. Comprehend the teaching objectives *kindness and gentleness.*

4. Show an increased ability to be kind and gentle.

5. Identify various types of seeds and define the word "gleaning."

Learning to be kind takes time and practice. In order to act gently and show kindness, a child must first experience a gentle touch and be shown kindness. You can help the children learn to be kind by remembering how children learn kindness at different ages and developmental stages.

How Children Learn to Be Kind

Age 3: A baby demonstrates empathy by crying in response to another baby's crying. Toddlers offer to share a cookie or a soothing pat on the back to comfort a sad playmate. At 3, a child can practice sharing and taking turns and be a great "helper" in the classroom. You can encourage, applaud, and model kind and helpful behaviors. Encourage each child to take turns, share toys, say thank you, and give of self and possessions. Remember, you are laying a foundation. 3-year-olds are still very self-focused and it will take a few more years of practice before kindness, helpfulness, and empathy are shown consistently.

Age 4: 4-year-olds feel a closeness to nature and other living things. They like animals and delight in feeding and taking care of them, even though it may be inconsistently. You can foster feelings of love and concern and reinforce actions of kindness when you help your 4-year-olds take care of a plant, animal, or another person. If an untended plant's leaves droop, point out the result of inattention and help water the plant. At 4, children can learn empathy and kindness through stories that explore feelings. Discuss how all the characters might be feeling in favorite preschool and Bible stories, and, as opportunities arise, compare those characters and feelings with real-life situations.

Age 5: At 5, children can remember the recent past, have great imaginations, and possess a repertoire of experiences. They can finally begin to understand compassion by imagining how another person feels, can remember a time when they felt a certain way, and can relate to situations because of similar experiences. You can help 5-year-olds practice kindness by explaining why. "We wait in line patiently so everyone can enjoy a turn." "We're collecting canned goods for our food pantry so all families can have a good dinner." At 5, they can focus on the feelings and needs of others, but when they are tired or hungry, they resort quickly to meeting their own needs and will need your gentle touch.

Teaching Activities

Decorating the Bible Memory Verse: Collage Fun

Materials Needed

- Copies of the Bible memory verse (page 30), one per child
- Stalks of wheat
- Seeds such as corn or barley
- Glue

What to Do

1. Set up for this art project following your normal procedure, putting the wheat stalks, seeds, glue, and Bible memory verse pages on the art table. Since preschoolers love to play with glue, limit their access to it by pouring manageable amounts onto a Styrofoam tray. Thin it with water and provide cotton swabs or small paintbrushes as applicators.

2. Show the children how to apply glue to their paper and put wheat stalks and seeds on the glue.

3. Let dry.

Teaching Gentleness

- Encourage the children to speak gently and kindly to each other when asking for something they need. Remind them that saying please and thank you are good ways to be kind and gentle.

- Show the children the stalks of wheat, kernels of corn, and barley seeds. Explain that Scripture is unclear as to which Ruth gleaned; the Bible only says that it was grain. God is love and shows us love as He provides us with many grains to bake bread, crackers, cake, and cookies.

- Are the children waiting patiently for their turn at the art table or to use a specific supply? If so, praise them for their patience. If not, urge them to remember Abraham and Sarah and to practice patience.

Keeping the Story Alive in the Classroom: Moving Day

Materials Needed

- Moving boxes
- Styrofoam peanuts
- Fragile items such as blown-out eggshells, Tinker toy constructions, puzzles, etc.

What to Do

1. Set up two "Moving Day Centers" in your classroom by placing the boxes, peanuts, and fragile items in one area and an empty spot (to represent Naomi's new house) in another.

2. Show the children how to pack a fragile (but not expensive or irreplaceable) item in the Styrofoam peanuts.

3. When the box is packed, have the children carry it carefully over to the new "house" and unpack it.

Teaching Gentleness

- Did the fragile item make the journey in one piece? Congratulate the packer on using a gentle technique.

- Encourage the children to work together on this project. Remind them to use gentle actions with each other as well as with the fragile objects. Did anyone say thank you or please? Praise that child for speaking gently and kindly just as Ruth did.

- As your children pack for the move, help them retell the story of Ruth. Speculate on the kind of things Ruth might have packed to take with her to a new country.

- This project can be quite messy, with Styrofoam peanuts all over the place. Some days it might require a lot of patience and kindness on your part to let the children continue "Moving Day." Remember, you are their model. Show them clearly what patience and gentleness mean.

Gentle Hugs: A Circle-Time Game to Teach Gentleness

Materials Needed

- Nothing special

What to Do

1. During Circle Time, select two children (or more, depending on the size of your class) to be "huggers." Have them move to the front of the room.

2. Tell the remaining children to turn their backs to the huggers and hide their eyes.

3. Have each hugger choose one child, coming up from behind quietly and giving a gentle hug to that child. Then, have the huggers return to the front of the room.

4. The children who were hugged try to guess who did the hugging. If they guess correctly, they get to take that hugger's spot up front.

5. Repeat until everyone has had a chance to be the hugger in this gentle variation of the familiar game, 7-Up.

Teaching Gentleness

- Remind the huggers that all hugs must be gentle. Have the children practice gentle hugs with each other before beginning the game. Contrast these loving touches (called hugs) with rough ones (called wrestling holds).

- After a few rounds, encourage the huggers to be kind and to hug someone who has not had a chance to be a hugger.

- Encourage kind responses from hugged children who guess incorrectly. If necessary, help them think of kind words to express their disappointment.

- Waiting to be hugged is so hard! Tiptoeing and moving quietly is tricky too! Praise the children for their Abraham-and-Sarah-like patience and perseverance.

Ruth's New House: An Art Project to Teach the Story

Materials Needed

- Several cardboard tubes from toilet paper, paper towels, wrapping paper, etc.

- A large sheet of strong cardboard (2' × 3') for the base

- Glue

- Paint

- Containers for paint

- Brushes

What to Do

1. Set up for this art project as normal. In the center of the art table, place the large sheet of cardboard. Be sure the children can reach the center of the base. Place the glue and tubes around the cardboard.

2. Show the children how to use lots of glue to attach the tubes to the cardboard base or to other tubes. Gently encourage them to make a house.

3. Let the structure dry completely overnight.

4. The next day, put the paint in the containers. Put the paint and the brushes around the tube-house structure. Help the children paint the house.

5. Let it dry and enjoy the creation.

Teaching Gentleness

- This activity encourages cooperation, a way of treating each other gently. Whenever you notice two or more children cooperating on this activity, compliment them on their behavior. Urge uncooperative students to use kind words and gentle actions with each other.

- Do you hear please and thank you being said? Praise the use of kind and gentle words!

- As hard as it is to be kind and gentle to others, it is often harder to be kind to ourselves. If one of the children is criticizing her own work, insist that gentle words be used. If a child learns to be gentle and kind to herself, she will be calmer and more self-assured. Struggling is okay; criticizing is not.

Sorting Seeds: A Center Activity to Teach the Story

Materials Needed

- Strips of cardboard, 3" × 12" each
- Marker
- 4–12 different kinds of large, sturdy seeds or beans
- Glue
- 1–3 small, covered containers (yogurt cups work well)

What to Do

1. Before school begins, divide each strip into four equal sections. Draw a solid line between the sections with the marker.

2. Glue one seed in the middle of each section. Label each section with the name of the seed.

3. Put the remaining seeds into a small container.

4. Show the children how to sort the seeds onto the appropriate section.

Teaching Gentleness

- Insist that the children clean up after this activity, returning the seeds to the appropriate small container. That way, it will be ready for the next child. Cleaning up after one's self is a way of treating others kindly.

- Ruth had to separate the grain from the chaff; sorting the seeds is a similar activity.

- Sorting seeds can be hard on little fingers. Remind the children to work patiently, just as Abraham and Sarah waited patiently for Isaac.

Gentle Blows: A Center Activity to Teach Gentleness

Materials Needed

- 2–3 table tennis balls
- 2–3 tennis balls
- Dishpan
- Water
- Small, plastic container

What to Do

1. Put all the balls in the small plastic container. Fill the dishpan with water. Put both items in the Activity Center.

2. Tell the children to put the balls in the dishpan. Show them how to blow the balls from one side of the dishpan to the other. Limit the number of blows each child may use.

3. After each child finishes blowing the balls, ask if the ball required gentle or hard blows to get it to move.

Teaching Gentleness

- This game illustrates the difference between gentle and hard. Once the children have sorted out the difference, ask them to describe a gentle touch (hugs, kisses, taps, pats) and a hard touch (hits, kicks, punches, pinches). Which do they prefer?

- Moving the tennis balls may be very hard for young lungs. Encourage the children to work together to blow the tennis balls across the water. Remind them that cooperation is an example of kind and gentle behavior.

- Prompt the children to retell the story of Ruth with questions like these: Who acted gently? Was gleaning the grain easy or hard work? Was it easy or hard for Ruth to leave her parents?

Balloon Blows: A Gentle Game to Teach the Memory Verse

Materials Needed

- Balloon

What to Do

1. Before Circle Time, inflate the balloon.

2. During Circle Time, have the class try to keep the balloon in the air by gently hitting it. Help the children to say one word of the Bible memory verse each time the balloon is tapped until the whole verse has been said.

3. Repeat this game several times.

Teaching Gentleness

- Encourage the children to be kind to one another by ensuring that everyone has a chance to hit the balloon at least once. Invite them to hit it to someone who has not had a chance to tap the balloon. Praise them for doing so.

- Encourage the children to say the Bible memory verse with you and to not yell out things such as, "Me! Me! Hit it to me!" Remind them yelling is not a gentle way to talk; demanding a turn is not gentle behavior. A normal voice is a gentle way to talk; cooperation and sharing are gentle behaviors.

- Connecting hand to balloon can be difficult for little ones. Encourage the children to be kind to themselves if they miss. Kindness must start from within.

- Preschoolers love repetition, so feel free to repeat any of the other suggestions for teaching gentleness from other activities.

Gentle Rain Stick: A Craft Project to Teach the Bible Memory Verse

Materials Needed

- Copies of the Gentle Rain Stick Bible memory verse (page 32), at least one per child
- Scissors, child-sized
- Cardboard paper towel or wrapping paper tubes, at least one per child
- Crayons
- Glue
- Rice
- Wax paper
- Rubber bands, two per tube

What to Do

1. Follow your normal procedure for arranging the materials. Set the Gentle Rain Stick Bible memory verse, scissors, crayons, and wrapping paper tubes on the art table.

2. Have the children cut out the Gentle Rain Stick Bible memory verse by cutting on the solid lines.

3. Let them decorate the wrapping paper tube with crayons. When they are finished, help them glue the Gentle Rain Stick Bible memory verse onto it.

4. Glue a square of wax paper onto one end of the tube; use a rubber band to secure it.

5. When the glue has dried, pour about ¼ cup of rice into the tube. Glue a second square of wax paper on the other end of the Gentle Rain Stick; use a rubber band to secure it. Let it dry.

6. Show your children how to gently turn the tube over and over, listening to the gentle sound the falling rice makes.

Teaching Gentleness

- When more than one child is working on this project, remind them to use gentle words and kind actions with each other. Praise every appropriate word and action.

- Read the Bible memory verse individually with the children. Help them repeat it with you—remember to say the book, chapter, and verse too! Then help the children retell the story by listing the many ways Ruth was kind to Naomi.

- Waiting and waiting and waiting for the glue to dry can seem like forever. Encourage patience by reminding the children of Abraham and Sarah. Can they remember whom the couple was waiting for?

Telling the Story

To tell the story for this unit, refresh your memory by reading the book of Ruth. Make copies of the Ruth Rebus Pictures (page 31). Color them if you wish. Glue the pictures onto poster board and laminate, if desired. As you read the words in bold type, hold up the appropriate card. Follow the instructions in italics.

Today I am going to tell you a story from the Bible about Ruth and her mother-in-law named Naomi. I need you to help me tell the story. Whenever I hold up a picture, I want you to say the name of the picture. Let's practice what the pictures mean. This one is *(hold up the picture of Ruth)* **Ruth; this one is** *(hold up the picture of Naomi)* **Naomi. This one is** *(hold up the picture of Orpah)* **Orpah, this one is** *(hold up the picture of Boaz)* **Boaz. This picture represents** *(hold up the picture of grain)* **grain and this one is** *(hold up the picture of bread)* **bread.** *Hold up the appropriate pictures.*

How many of you know your grandmother? How many of you know your grandmother's grandmother? *Count hands.* Not too many of you. Well, today we are going to hear a story about Jesus' grandmother's grandmother's grandmother and so on, back 29 generations. Her name was *(hold up the picture of Ruth)* **Ruth**.

(Hold up the picture of Naomi) **Naomi** was married and had two sons. *(Hold up the picture of Naomi)* **Naomi** and her husband and sons had moved away from their families and lived in a foreign country. Her sons married two girls named *(hold up the picture of Orpah)* **Orpah and Ruth.** *(Hold up the picture of Ruth)* **Naomi's** husband died; then both of her sons died. *(Hold up the picture of Naomi)* **Naomi** decided to go back to the country where she had lived as a child, so she told *(hold up the picture of Orpah)* **Orpah** and *(hold up the picture of Ruth)* **Ruth** to go back home to their parents. *(Hold up the picture of Orpah)* **Orpah** obeyed but *(hold up the picture of Ruth)* **Ruth** would not go. She wanted to stay with *(hold up the picture of Naomi)* **Naomi** to take care of her.

(Hold up the picture of Ruth) **Ruth** and *(hold up the picture of Naomi)* **Naomi** walked to the country where *(hold up the picture of Naomi)* **Naomi** was born and stayed in her old house. *(Hold up the picture of Ruth)* **Ruth** helped *(hold up the picture of Naomi)* **Naomi** by cleaning and cooking. She did the shopping and the mending. All the neighbors thought *(hold up the picture of Ruth)* **Ruth** was very kind. Then one day, the two women ran out of food and money.

(Hold up the picture of Ruth) **Ruth** didn't want *(hold up the picture of Naomi)* **Naomi** to be hungry, so she went out into the fields and picked up the *(hold up the picture of grain)* **grain** that was left over after the harvest. She brought the *(hold up the picture of grain)* **grain** home and made *(hold up the picture of bread)* **bread** from it. She always let *(hold up the picture of Naomi)* **Naomi** eat first because *(hold up the picture of Ruth)* **Ruth** had a very kind heart.

(Hold up the picture of Naomi) **Naomi's** cousin *(hold up the picture of Boaz)*, **Boaz**, saw how hard *(hold up the picture of Ruth)* **Ruth** worked. He saw how kind she was to *(hold up the picture of Naomi)* **Naomi**. He told his servants to leave extra *(hold up the picture of grain)* **grain** in the fields for *(hold up the picture of Ruth)* **Ruth** to pick up so that *(hold up the picture of Naomi)* **Naomi** would have enough *(hold up the picture of bread)* **bread** to eat. Because *(hold up the picture of Ruth)* **Ruth** had been so gentle and kind to *(hold up the picture of Naomi)* **Naomi**, *(hold up the picture of Boaz)* **Boaz** was extra kind to her.

(Hold up the picture of Boaz) **Boaz** soon learned to love the kind woman *(hold up the picture of Ruth)*, **Ruth.** He married her. *(Hold up the picture of Ruth)* **Ruth** and *(hold up the picture of Boaz)* **Boaz** asked *(hold up the picture of Naomi)* **Naomi** to live with them so that *(hold up the picture of Ruth)* **Ruth** could take care of her. God chose *(hold up the picture of Ruth)* **Ruth** to be one of Jesus' ancestors. God loves it when we are kind and gentle.

Bible Memory Verse

Be kind … to one another.

Ephesians 4:32 (NIV)

Telling the Story - Rebus Pictures

Ruth

Grain

Naomi

Orpah

Bread

Boaz

Gentle Rain Stick Bible Memory Verse

Be kind ... to one another.

Ephesians 4:32 (NIV)

Dear Parent(s),

"Please be kind!" You began teaching gentleness when you first held your baby gently in your arms. Later, you told your crawling, exploring baby to be gentle as she touched something fragile. You want your child to develop a gentle touch into feelings and acts of kindness as she grows older. You often look for ways to teach your child to reach out and offer a helping hand to others. Ruth took care of and helped Naomi as they moved together to a new home. The farmer, Boaz, who purposely left grain in the fields for Ruth to glean, also reached out in kindness.

The lessons of Ruth and her kindness shouldn't stop at the classroom door. I invite you to share these lessons with your child at home by reading the story of Ruth from a preschool Bible, trying the activities provided in this letter, and teaching this Bible memory verse.

Be kind … to one another. *Ephesians 4:32*

Learning to be kind takes time and practice. In order to act gently and show kindness, a child must experience a gentle touch and be shown kindness. You can help your child learn to be kind by knowing how children learn kindness at different ages.

How Children Learn to Be Kind

Age 3: A baby demonstrates empathy by crying in response to another baby's crying. Toddlers offer to share a cookie or a soothing pat on the back to comfort a sad playmate. At 3, a child can practice sharing and taking turns and be a great "helper" in the classroom. You can encourage, applaud, and model kind and helpful behaviors. Encourage your child to take turns, share toys, say thank you, and give of self and possessions. Remember, you are laying a foundation. 3-year-olds are still very self-focused and it will take a few more years of practice before kindness, helpfulness, and empathy are shown consistently.

Age 4: 4-year-olds feel a closeness to nature and other living things. They like animals and delight in feeding and taking care of them, even though it may be inconsistently. You can foster feelings of love and concern and reinforce actions of kindness when you help your 4-year-old take care of a plant, animal, or another person. If an untended plant's leaves droop, point out the result of inattention and help water the plant. At 4, children can learn empathy and kindness through stories that explore feelings. Discuss how all the characters might be feeling in favorite preschool and Bible stories, and, as opportunities arise, compare those characters and feelings with real-life situations.

Age 5: At 5, children can remember the recent past, have great imaginations, and possess a repertoire of experiences. They can finally begin to understand compassion by imagining how another person feels, can remember a time when they felt a certain way, and can relate to situations because of similar experiences. You can help 5-year-olds practice kindness by explaining why. "We wait in line patiently so everyone can enjoy a turn." "We're collecting canned goods for our

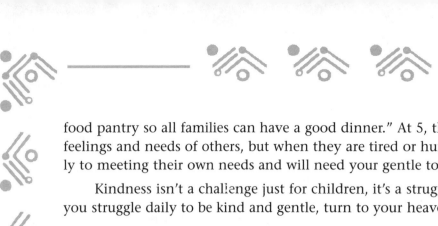

food pantry so all families can have a good dinner." At 5, they can focus on the feelings and needs of others, but when they are tired or hungry, they resort quickly to meeting their own needs and will need your gentle touch.

Kindness isn't a challenge just for children, it's a struggle for parents too. As you struggle daily to be kind and gentle, turn to your heavenly Father in prayer.

Parent's Prayer

Heavenly Father, Ruth was kind and cared for Naomi. Help me to model the same kind, helpful love for my child so she may understand Your love and, in turn, offer it to others. In Jesus' name I pray. Amen.

Together in Christ,

Family Activities

Gentle Clouds: A Cooking Adventure

Ingredients

- Your child's favorite flavor of pudding
- Your child's favorite fruit, cut into bite-sized pieces

What to Do

1. Help your child fill a small cup or bowl with pudding.
2. Show how to scatter fruit across the top.
3. Help your child share the treat with a sibling, friend, or parent.

Teaching Gentleness

- Show your child how to gently scatter some of the fruit on top of the pudding, then demonstrate how to vigorously throw some of the fruit on the pudding. Which looks best? Which is most gentle? Urge your child to be gentle with the fruit.

- Sharing is an action that shows kindness. Praise your child for sharing the pudding treat.

- Help your child retell the story of Ruth by asking questions such as: Who acted gently? (Ruth) Who made the food in the story? (Ruth) What kind of food was it? (Bread) Was it easy or hard for Ruth to glean the grain to make the bread? (Hard)

Ruth and Naomi Walkers: A Quiet-Time Game

Materials Needed

- Construction paper
- Ruler
- Pencil
- Scissors
- Crayons or markers
- Smooth, flat surface

What to Do

1. Using the ruler and the pencil, draw two 1″ × 5″ rectangles on the construction paper.

2. Depending on your child's skill with scissors, help cut out the rectangles.

3. Use the crayons or markers to decorate the rectangles. You might want to draw a woman on each rectangle to represent Ruth and Naomi. Let your child color the women.

4. Use the edge of the ruler to curl the rectangles slightly, as if you were curling ribbon. (See diagram.)

5. Place the Ruth and Naomi "walkers" on the smooth, flat surface. Blow gently on their heads and watch them walk across the surface.

Teaching Gentleness

- Encourage your child to blow gently but firmly on the walkers. If blown too hard, the pictures will fly through the air. That wouldn't be very kind, would it?

- At least once, be sure to send the Naomi walker across the surface first, just as Ruth followed Naomi. Help your child retell the story by asking these questions: Who left first? (Naomi) Who followed Naomi? (Ruth) Did Naomi tell Ruth to return home? (Yes) What did Ruth say? (Wherever you go, Naomi, I will go too.)

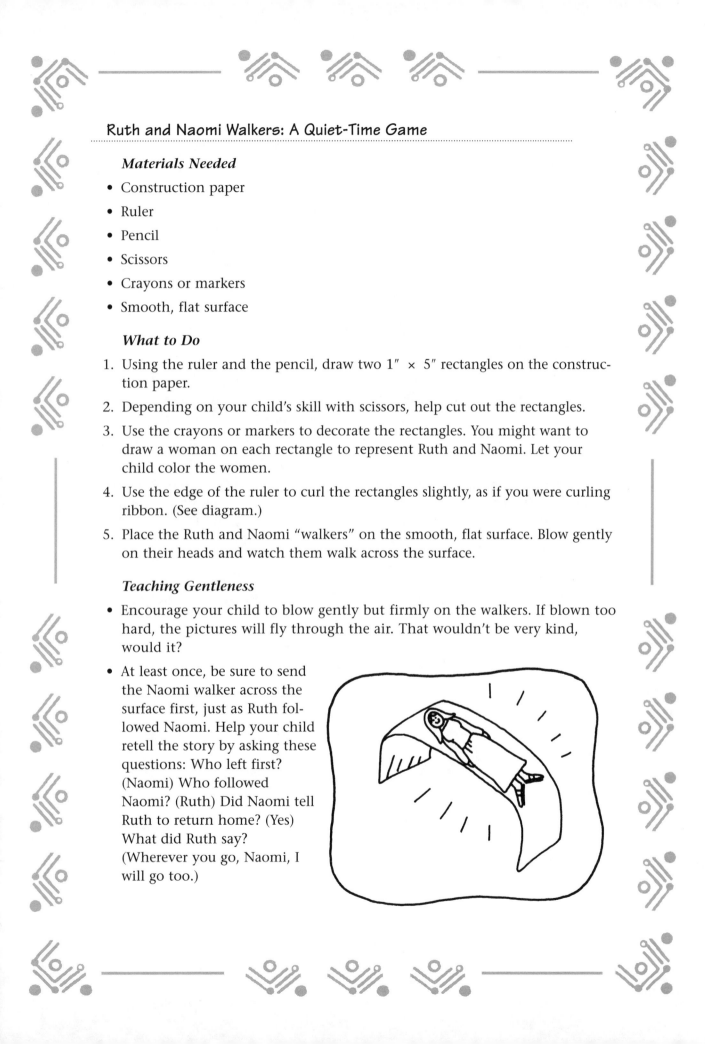

Setting the Table: A Helping Task

Materials Needed

- Patience
- A complete place setting for each family member

What to Do

1. Select a quiet time in the day's routine to teach your child how to set the table. Try to choose a time away from the hustle and bustle of the dinner hour. Show how to place the plate, arrange the silverware, fold the napkin, etc. For younger children, just teach how to place the silverware.

Teaching Gentleness

- Children can feel like a useful part of the family by doing household chores. This is a simple chore that children as young as 3 can learn—and you are doing them a kindness by helping them contribute to the household.

- Even plastic dishes can be broken with harsh treatment. Encourage your child to handle the things gently so that nothing gets broken.

- After your child has mastered this task, help him retell the story of Ruth by asking these questions: Who probably set the table in Naomi's house? (Ruth) What do you think they had to eat? (bread, cheese, fresh fruit, olives) Did Ruth act kindly? (Yes) Why? (Because it helped Naomi.)

Other Simple Ideas

1. Play "Wink at Me" at the dinner table. Teach your child how to wink and then to look you in the eye during dinner time, searching for a wink. Looking someone in the eye when speaking helps convey friendliness and kindness. Encourage your child to look others in the eye too.

Be a Friend!

David and Jonathan Are Friends

Bible Memory Verse

A friend loves at all times. *Proverbs 17:17*

Teacher's Prayer

Heavenly Father, You sent Your Son, Jesus, to be my best friend. As my friend, He always listens to my joys and sorrows, accepts me unconditionally, forgives my failings, shares my interests, teaches, guides, and protects me. Help me to give the gift of friendship to the children, that by this gift, they will know You and learn to give and receive friendship many times over during their lives. In Jesus' name I pray. Amen.

Teaching Objective: Friendship

To help children learn to be friends, just as David and Jonathan were good friends.

Through God's Word and the power of the Holy Spirit, by the end of this unit, the children should be able to:

1. Tell the basic story of David and Jonathan.

2. Repeat the Bible memory verse.

3. Comprehend the teaching objective *friendship*.

4. Show an increased ability to be friendly.

5. Identify a quiver and an arrow.

Learning to be a friend takes time and practice. In order to be a friend, a child must first see friendship in action. Adult models of thoughtfulness, support, caring, and shared interests are a foundation on which children can build their own friendships. You can foster friendships and teach friendly behavior by recognizing and remembering how children develop friendships at different ages.

How Children Learn to Be Friends

Age 3: At 3, children define friends as almost anyone they play with regularly. They are just learning to interact with others. They move from side-by-side, noninteractive play to the give-and-take of exploratory play. They explore how to relate to peers. Part of this exploration includes testing limits, sharing, hugging, and anger. As 3-year-olds learn to interact, there are many opportunities to reinforce sharing, patience, and gentleness, while accepting that disagreements, hurt feelings, and frustration are a normal part of the learning process.

Age 4: A 4-year-old chooses friends who share similar interests and enjoy similar activities. "Robin and I are friends; we both like to build with blocks." "Josh and I are best friends; we ride trikes faster than anybody." They are better at using words instead of hands to express their feelings and desires, but their verbal ability in conflict resolution is often expressed in name-calling or statements like, "You're not my friend anymore." Suggest alternative words while recognizing and accepting the attempts at verbal communication. 4-year-olds retain some of the possessiveness of earlier stages, saying, "He's MY friend," and don't understand that someone can be friends with many people at the same time.

Age 5: 5-year-olds are better playmates than they were at ages 3 and 4 because of their desire to cooperate. Respect their abilities, and refrain from intervening in their attempts to solve problems or resolve conflicts. At 5, children enjoy similar interests and activities with friends, but they also teach each other new skills and inspire confidence by saying, "Come on, Michael, slide down the pole. I did it, and you can do it too."

Teaching Activities

Keeping the Teaching Objective Alive in the Classroom: Friendly Fire

Materials Needed

- Copies of the Empty Quivers (page 45), one per child
- Scissors, child-sized
- Markers
- Straws, approximately 5 per child
- Copies of Arrowheads and Feathers (page 46), one set per child
- straw
- Clear tape
- Crayons
- Masking tape

What to Do

1. Cut out the copies of the Empty Quivers.
2. Use the marker to label each quiver with a child's name.
3. Cut out the arrowheads and feathers.
4. Use the scissors to cut a small slit in one end of each straw. Slide an arrowhead into each slit. Secure it with clear tape.
5. Tape feathers to the opposite end of each straw.
6. Let the children decorate their quiver with crayons. Use the masking tape to tape each quiver to the wall.
7. During Circle Time, show the children the "Friendly Arrows" made from the straws. Explain to the children that each

time a child does something friendly, the recipient of the kindness can put an arrow into the friendly child's quiver.

Teaching Friendship

- Encourage the children to remember the friendly actions that earned the arrows so they can share their accomplishments during Circle Time. Share praise and affirmation for each kindness, helping others to share words of encouragement as well.

- Did the recipients of the friendly behavior say thank you? If not, urge them to do so. Saying thank you is another way to be a friend.

- Be sure to point out and reward friendly behaviors. Focus on behaviors the young child might not see as ways of being a friend: smiling, looking one another in the eye, helping, using kind words, being tolerant of one's own mistakes, etc. Model the behaviors you expect and reward these behaviors when you see them.

Decorating the Bible Memory Verse: A Pulled Print to Share

Materials Needed

- Large plastic shower curtain or drop cloth
- 1–3 old cookie sheet(s)
- Washable tempera paint
- Small paint cups
- Spoons
- Copies of the Bible memory verse (page 44), at least one per child

What to Do

1. Set up for this art project as normal. Cover the work surface with the large plastic shower curtain or drop cloth,

placing the cookie sheets on top. Fill the small paint cups about half-full with washable tempera paint, and put a spoon in each cup.

2. Direct the children to the art table in pairs. Show them how to use the spoons to dribble paint directly onto the cookie sheets. Allow them to smoosh the paint around with their fingers or hands.

3. When the pair of children is satisfied with its masterpiece, help them wash and dry their hands.

4. Help them gently press a copy of the Bible memory verse, word-side down, on top of the painted surface. Rub lightly back and forth over the paper. Peel the paper from the cookie sheet. Make second and third prints from the same masterpiece.

Teaching Friendship

- It is entirely possible that the words of the memory verse will be obliterated by the pulled print. This is perfectly acceptable. It is the process of creating the painting together that forms friendships, not the words on the page. When dry, the words can be re-printed on the page.

- Ask the children to tell how they helped each other and showed love in this project. Help them understand how they have lived out this verse by working together.

- Compare the finished prints. What is the same? What is different? Help the children see that it is the uniqueness of each person that makes friendship special.

- Help the children retell the story by asking how David and Jonathan worked together (making a plan, agreeing on a secret signal).

Friends Make Room: a Circle-Time Game to Teach Friendliness

Materials Needed

- Full sheets of newspaper, one per child
- A source of music

What to Do

1. Fold the newspaper sheets into quarters. Arrange the folded newspapers in a circle on the floor.

2. Have each child stand on a sheet of newspaper. Explain that you are going to play "Friends Make Room," a game like musical chairs. The difference is no one will be eliminated because more than one person can stand on a piece of newspaper!

3. Start the music and have them walk in a circle. Stop the music and make sure each child is standing on a piece of newspaper.

4. Have two children team up as buddies and remove one piece of newspaper.

5. Repeat until all the children are piled on one sheet of newspaper. You may need to unfold the newspapers to make them larger, accommodating more children. Remove more than one sheet of newspaper each round if you want the game to go faster.

Teaching Friendship

- Friends share. Praise the children as they share newspapers and help their friends fit into the small space, reinforcing the concept of friendship.

- Encourage the children to help each other find room on the newspaper. If one child is standing alone, unsure of where to go, encourage others to invite him onto their paper. Thank the children for these friendly gestures. Help the children to say thank you to each other as well.

- Jonathan went out of his way to help his friend David. Compliment those who go out of their way to help their classmates.

- Model this friendliness yourself if you join the game. Help the children step onto your paper and thank them when they invite you onto theirs.

Friendship Sculpture: An Art Project to Teach Friendliness

Materials Needed

- A large sheet of sturdy cardboard or plywood

- Assorted recyclable materials: boxes, yogurt cups, string, sticks, empty film canisters, yarn, plastic lids, frozen juice lids, etc.

- Glue

- Newspapers

What to Do

1. Spread newspaper on the art table. Put the large sheet of cardboard or plywood in the center. Place the glue and recyclable materials around the sides.

2. Direct the children to work on the project in small groups or, if you prefer, have the whole class work on the sculpture at one time. Show them how to glue the materials to the base first and then to other materials. Use lots of glue.

3. Let the sculpture dry. Display it in a prominent place. Add a label indicating the names of the friends who worked together to create the masterpiece.

Teaching Friendship

- Are the children sharing the materials? Praise them for their friendly actions, and remind them that David and Jonathan shared many things as friends.

- Encourage the children to help each other, just like David and Jonathan. Friends help each other.

- Talk about the materials. Explain that recycling this "trash" is a way of being friendly to the earth.

Friendship Puzzles: A Center Activity to Teach Friendliness

Materials Needed

- Puzzles that fit into a bottom frame

- 2 resealable plastic bags for each puzzle

- Brown lunch bags, one per puzzle

What to Do

1. Set up a puzzle center. Divide the pieces from each puzzle into the two resealable bags. Place each pair of plastic bags into a lunch bag, labeled with a brief description of the puzzle. Store in an easily accessible place. Put the empty puzzle frames in the puzzle center.

2. When a child goes to the puzzle center, explain that the pieces are missing. Assure her that you will provide the pieces if she can find a friend to work with her.

3. Let the pair of children select a puzzle. Get the matching lunch bag, giving one plastic bag of pieces to each child. Encourage them to work together as they complete the puzzle.

4. When finished, help the children sort the puzzle pieces, placing them in the separate plastic bags and returning them to the brown lunch bag.

Teaching Friendship

- Some of the children might be very shy. When appropriate, praise a shy child for having the courage to approach a class-mate and ask him to do this activity. Coach this interaction, if necessary, to ensure success.

- Watch as the children work together. Comment on friendly words and actions. Encourage them to continue working together in a friendly fashion until all the puzzles have been completed.

- Friends share, take turns, and help each other. Reward friendly behaviors with words of encouragement. After all, encouragement is another way to be a friend!

Friends Stick Together: A Center Activity to Teach the Story

Materials Needed

- 10 different pieces of wallpaper
- Scissors, child-sized
- A gingerbread person cookie cutter (optional)
- Pencil
- Small basket
- Clear, sticky paper
- Masking tape

What to Do

1. Using the gingerbread cookie cutter as a pattern, cut out ten pairs of gingerbread friends, one pair from each piece of wallpaper.

2. Scramble the pairs, putting them in the basket.

3. Tape the clear, sticky paper, sticky-side out, to a table top or wall. Set the basket beside the sticky paper.

4. Have the children match the ginger-bread friends and place them together on the sticky paper.

Teaching Friendship

- Friends often have things in common such as activities, likes and dislikes, etc. As the children match pairs, help them think of things they have in common with friends.

- Ask the children what they think it means for friends to "stick together." Help them understand that it does not mean friends are glued together or stay with each other all the time. Explain that it means friends will be dependable and supportive.

- Are the children using kind words with each other? Are they waiting patiently? If not, help them remember the stories of Ruth and Naomi, Abraham and Sarah. Help them put kindness and patience into practice as a way of being a friend.

Blanket Ball: An Outdoor Game to Teach the Bible Memory Verse

Materials Needed

- Copy of the Bible memory verse (page 44)
- 2 balls
- 2 beach towels
- Plenty of room

What to Do

1. Read the Bible memory verse aloud. Talk about what it means.

2. Divide the children into two teams, assigning one adult per team. Give each team a ball and a beach towel.

3. Have the children hold onto an edge or a corner of their team's towel. Place the ball on the beach towel. Work together to toss and roll the ball around on the beach towel.

4. When the teams have practiced, toss the ball into the air, saying one word of the Bible memory verse with each toss. Be sure to say the chapter and verse too!

5. Older children, or those especially coordinated, might want to toss one ball back and forth between the towels, saying each word of the Bible memory verse each time.

Teaching Friendship

• Cooperation is a friendly behavior. Urge the children to cooperate as they say the verse and be friends.

• If the ball falls off the beach towel, say, "That's all right!" and "Let's try again." Be sure to forgive yourself for such "failures" with words such as "I'll try harder!" or "Oops! It's OK for me to make a mistake." Friendship starts with liking and accepting one's self.

• Tossing the ball back and forth promotes consideration and taking turns. Point out that these are friendly behaviors and, just as the verse says, they are good behaviors to use at all times.

Friendship Vest: A Craft Project to Teach the Bible Memory Verse

Materials Needed

• Brown grocery bags, one for each child
• Scissors, adult- and child-sized
• Markers
• Construction paper
• Glue
• Newspapers

What to Do

1. Follow the diagram below to cut out a Friendship Vest for each child. Use the marker to write the Bible memory verse on the back of each vest.

2. Set out the vests, child-sized scissors, markers, construction paper, and glue.

3. Show how to cut interesting shapes from the construction paper and glue them onto the vest.

Teaching Friendship

• Read the Bible memory verse individually with the children. Ask them how they might show love. List other friendly behaviors.

• Encourage the children to share their friendship vest with another friend. Explain that sharing, or giving, is a friendly thing to do.

• As the children work, are they using kind words? If so, praise them. If not, remind them of Ruth and her actions. Are they waiting patiently for materials? If so, praise this friendly behavior. If not, remind them how Abraham and Sarah waited patiently.

Telling the Story

To tell the story for this unit, first refresh your memory by reading 1 Samuel 20:1–20, 42. Create a book by copying the pictures on pages 47–52, making one copy for yourself, and one for every two children in your class. Make a construction paper cover, adding the title "David and Jonathan, True Friends." Staple the pages together down the lefthand side to form a simple book. Decorate with bright colors. You will also need a bell to ring and pairs of stickers or ink stamps to place on the children's hands. Gather the children at your feet and tell the following story. Read the words in bold print while you follow the directions in italics.

Everybody hold out your left hand. *Check to make sure the left hands are extended.* **I am going to place a sticker (or stamp) on each left hand.** *Do so.* **Stand up. Now find the person with the sticker that matches yours. When you have found your partner, sit down together.** *Wait until all the children are seated again, checking the stickers for matches as they do so.* **Now we are going to hear about a pair of friends named David and Jonathan. I will read from my book while each pair of friends shares a book. When I ring the bell, it will be time to turn the page.** *Hand out the books, giving one to each pair.* **This story is from the Bible. The title is "David and Jonathan, True Friends."** *Ring the bell. Be sure that each book is opened to the first page.*

David and Jonathan were best friends, as close as brothers. In fact, David married Jonathan's sister. But, King Saul, Jonathan's father, did not like David. King Saul tried to kill David. *Ring the bell and turn the page. Be sure that all the children have turned their pages.*

King Saul sent men to David's house to kill him the next morning. David's wife said, **"Run for your life tonight, or tomorrow you'll be killed." So David climbed out through a window, and he escaped.** *Ring the bell and turn the page.*

David went to Jonathan and asked, "What have I done wrong? Why is your father trying to kill me?" "He is afraid that you will be king," Jonathan said to David. "But I am your best friend and I want to help you."

David said, "I am invited to eat dinner with the king, but I will hide in this field instead. Tell the king that I went home to visit my family. If King Saul says, 'Very well,' then you will know that I am safe. But if he gets angry, you will know that he wants to kill me." Then David and Jonathan decided on a secret way for Jonathan to warn David of King Saul's plans. *Ring the bell and turn the page.*

David hid in the field, waiting for his best friend Jonathan. *Ring the bell and turn the page.*

Jonathan came to the field and shot three arrows at a big stone. "Look," cried Jonathan loudly to his servant. "The arrows went past the stone." That was the secret signal to David that King Saul was going to hurt him. *Ring the bell and turn the page.*

David would have to run away. He wanted to say good-bye to Jonathan. David bowed down before Jonathan three times. Then they kissed each other and cried. Jonathan said to David, "Go in peace, for we are friends with each other in the name of the Lord." Then David left, and Jonathan went back home. *Close the book. You have finished the story.*

Bible Memory Verse

A friend loves
at all times.

Proverbs 17:17 (NIV)

Empty Quivers

Arrowheads and Feathers

Telling the Story, page 1

Telling the Story, page 3

Telling the Story, page 4

Telling the Story, page 5

Telling the Story, page 6

Dear Parent(s),

"Be a friend." Friends like to do the same things. Friends like and accept you, and being together brings happiness. Friends make a child feel special. Friendship starts at home, talking together, sharing activities, being patient, having fun. Through these, a child learns the basics of friendship. When ready to reach out to others his own age, these social skills will help your child be a friend. Peer friendships provide relationships that parents and siblings just can't provide.

This month our class will learn about David and Jonathan and their very special friendship. David and Jonathan were best friends, sharing possessions, enjoying each other's company, and protecting each other. We will emphasize the importance of being a friend and the special blessing of our best friend, Jesus. The lessons of David and Jonathan and friendship shouldn't stop at the classroom door. Share these lessons with your child at home by reading the story of David and Jonathan from a preschool Bible, trying the activities provided in this letter, and teaching this Bible memory verse.

A friend loves at all times. *Proverbs 17:17*

Learning to be a friend takes time and practice. In order to be a friend, a child must first see friendship in action. Adult models of thoughtfulness, support, caring, and shared interests are a foundation on which children can build their own friendships. Help your child learn to be a friend by understanding how children practice friendship at different ages.

How Children Learn to Be Friends

Age 3: At 3, children define friends as almost anyone they play with regularly. They are just learning to interact with others. They move from side-by-side, noninteractive play to the give-and-take of exploratory play. They explore how to relate to peers. Part of this exploration includes testing limits, sharing, hugging, and anger. As 3-year-olds learn to interact, there are many opportunities to reinforce sharing, patience, and gentleness, while accepting that disagreements, hurt feelings, and frustration are a normal part of the learning process.

Age 4: A 4-year-old chooses friends who share similar interests and enjoy similar activities. "Robin and I are friends; we both like to build with blocks." "Josh and I are best friends; we ride trikes faster than anybody." They are better at using words instead of hands to express their feelings and desires, but their verbal ability in conflict resolution is often expressed in name-calling or statements like, "You're not my friend anymore." Suggest alternative words while recognizing and accepting the attempts at verbal communication. 4-year-olds retain some of the possessiveness of earlier stages, saying, "He's MY friend," and don't understand that someone can be friends with many people at the same time.

Age 5: 5-year-olds are better playmates than they were at ages 3 and 4 because of their desire to cooperate. Respect their abilities, and refrain from intervening in their attempts to solve problems or resolve conflicts. At 5, children enjoy similar interests and activities with friends, but they also teach each other new skills and inspire confidence by saying, "Come on, Michael, slide down the pole. I did it, and you can do it too."

Parent's Prayer

Heavenly Father, You sent Your Son, Jesus, to be my best friend. As my friend, He always listens to my joys and sorrows, accepts me unconditionally, forgives my failings, shares my interests, teaches, guides, and protects me. Help me to give the gift of friendship to my child, that by this gift, he will know You and might learn to give and receive friendship many times over during his life. In Jesus' name I pray. Amen

Together in Christ,

Family Activities

Bear Cream: A Cooking Adventure

Ingredients

- 1–2 bananas
- ½ cup berries or other fruit
- 1 cup orange juice
- Knife
- Cookie sheet
- Blender
- 1 glass
- 2 straws

What to Do

1. Help your child peel the banana and slice it into 1" chunks. Place the chunks on the cookie sheet.

2. Together, wash the berries or other fruit. Cut them into bite-sized pieces and place them on the cookie sheet.

3. Place the cookie sheet in the freezer for about an hour or until the fruit is firm, but not frozen solid.

4. Remove the fruit from the freezer and pour it into a blender. Help your child pour the orange juice into the blender.

5. Whirl the mixture until it is smooth and creamy. Pour it into the glass, add the straws, and share a creamy treat!

Teaching Friendship

- Friends share. Encourage your child to think of someone with whom she could share this treat: you, a sibling, or a neighbor. Help her plan and carry out ways to share this treat—that's what good friends do.

- Friendship is a healthy sweet treat, just like this drink. Explain how wonderful it feels to have a good friend—almost as wonderful as this creamy drink!

- Is your child finding it hard to wait for the fruit to freeze? Pass the time by retelling the story, asking these questions: Who were the two friends who shared? (David and Jonathan) Who was trying to hurt David? (King Saul, Jonathan's father) How did David get away from King Saul the first time? (He climbed out a window of his house.)

Friendship Cups: A Craft Project

Materials Needed

- 2 small glasses or clear plastic pots
- 2–3 colors of tempera paint
- Glue
- 2–3 small paint containers
- 4–6 cotton swabs
- Newspapers
- Clear, nonyellowing, nontoxic varnish or other sealer

What to Do

1. Cover the work surface with newspapers.
2. Pour tempera paint into each of the paint containers. Mix glue into the paint, making it thick.
3. Use the cotton swabs to paint a design on the glasses. Wipe off mistakes with a paper towel before drying. Be sure to paint only the outside of the glass.
4. Let the cups dry. To preserve the finished design, cover it with a coat of clear sealer.
5. Keep one of the cups and share the other with a friend!

Teaching Friendship

- Teach your child the fine art of giving and receiving compliments. Help him think of one nice thing to say to you about working together on this activity. Be sure to pay your young artist a sincere compliment. Then coach your child to simply say thank you and not brush off the compliment. Giving compliments is a way of being friends with others; graciously receiving them is a way of being friends with one's self.

- While painting, help your child retell the story of David and Jonathan by asking these questions: How did Jonathan help David? (By telling him that King Saul planned to kill him) Where did David wait to find out about this? (In a deserted field) How did Jonathan give David the bad news? (By shooting three arrows)

Friendly Fish: A Game to Play

Materials Needed

- Construction paper
- Scissors, child-sized
- Marker
- Paper clips
- Magnet (a refrigerator magnet will work just fine)
- Stick
- String
- Bucket

What to Do

1. Cut simple fish shapes from the construction paper. With your child, write the name of a friend on each fish.

2. Attach several paper clips to each fish.

3. Assemble a fishing pole. Tie the string on one end of the stick, and tie the magnet to the end of the string, like a "hook."

4. Put the fish in the bucket.

5. Go fishing. As each fish is caught, read the name written on it. Help your child say a simple prayer for that friend. Now think of ways to show friendship to that person. Follow through on some of these ideas!

Teaching Friendship

- Include the names of siblings or other family members on the fish. Friends and playmates may come and go, but a sibling, parent, or other relative is a friend for life. Encourage your child to view siblings as friends and to treat the sibling accordingly.

- Include the child's own name on one of the fish. After all, a child who learns to be good friends with himself grows up to be less stressed, lonely, and depressed and more self-confident, friendly, and satisfied with life.

Other Simple Ideas

1. Be extra nice and friendly this month. Your child will see this model and copy it. For friendship to be important to your child, she must see that it is important to you. Call a friend, invite a friend to visit, or send a postcard to a friend.

2. Smile at your child and at others. Friendly people smile.

3. Strive to show good manners. Friendly people are polite people.

I'm Sorry!

Mary Is Forgiven

Bible Memory Verse

Your sins are forgiven. *Mark 2:5*

Teacher's Prayer

Heavenly Father, You sent Your only Son to die on the cross to pay for my sins, and I come to you many times each day, penitent and asking for forgiveness. Help me accept the failures of my children with the same loving forgiveness and guidance You give to me. In Jesus' name I pray. Amen.

Teaching Objective: Forgiveness

To help children learn to ask for and accept forgiveness, just as Mary knew Jesus as her Savior and asked for and received forgiveness for her sins.

Through God's Word and the power of the Holy Spirit, by the end of this unit, the children should be able to:

1. Tell the basic story of Mary.

2. Repeat the Bible memory verse.

3. Comprehend the teaching objective *repentance and forgiveness.*

4. Show an increased ability to say, "I'm sorry."

5. Identify the difference between accidental and purposeful wrongs.

Learning to ask for, accept, and offer forgiveness takes time and practice. You can help children learn about forgiveness by first knowing how children understand forgiveness at different ages.

How Children Learn about Forgiveness

Age 3: A 3-year-old will say the words, "I'm sorry," when she knows she has broken a rule or hurt a friend. Sometimes she will say the words without prompting from an adult, but more often she will need a gentle reminder. At 3, they are just beginning to recognize the way someone else might feel and the impact of their actions on others. You can help the children understand apologies and forgiveness by setting a good example. When you lose your temper or fail to keep a promise, remember to say "I'm sorry." When she tells you that she made a mistake and is sorry, remember to say, "I forgive you." Tell her that Jesus loves her with all her faults and failings, and you do too. Continue to teach through your good example that asking for forgiveness is a rewarding experience.

Age 4: 4-year-olds are becoming aware of "good" and "bad." They may become more spontaneous in prayer, asking God to help them be good. Help them understand the difference between accidental and intentional wrongs. "You didn't mean to spill the paint. The ball accidentally hit the easel. But you chose to break our rule—no ball bouncing in the classroom." Establish a few important classroom rules, explain the reasons for these rules, set forth consequences for breaking the rules, and remain calm and matter-of-fact when enforcing them. 4-year-olds can begin to connect the "badness" of breaking a rule with the bad feelings connected to failure and the good feelings connected to apologies and forgiveness.

Age 5: At 5, children can better understand the concepts of confession, "I did something wrong and I'm sorry"; and absolution, "You have forgiven me and we will start again fresh." Use every opportunity to point out these components in daily encounters with friends, family members, Bible and storybook characters, and TV presentations. When you must point out a child's transgression, do it as quietly and privately as possible. It is easier to apologize and receive forgiveness when not embarrassed by the presence of others.

Teaching Activities

Decorate the Bible Memory Verse: Resisting Artwork

Materials Needed

- Copies of the Bible memory verse (page 64), one per child
- White crayons
- Watercolors
- Containers of water
- Brushes

What to Do

1. Follow normal procedure for set up and put the white crayons on the art table. Add the containers of water, brushes, and watercolors.

2. Show the children how to draw with the white crayon on their Bible memory verse papers. It can be an abstract drawing or a picture of something.

3. When they have finished drawing, have them paint over the entire picture with the watercolors. The wax from the crayon markings will show through.

Teaching Repentance

- Say the Bible memory verse aloud with each child. Explain that Jesus forgives and how important it is to forgive others. No matter what, Jesus keeps loving each and every one.

- Explain to the children that the paint could not cover the white crayon spots on the picture. Where Jesus is, no sin can stick.

- Should a mishap happen with the art supplies, encourage the child to ask for forgiveness. Help him find the right words to express repentance.

- Are your children waiting patiently for their turn? Praise them for being like Abraham and Sarah. Are they using kind words? Praise them for being like Ruth. Are they acting friendly? Compliment them for acting like David and Jonathan. Praise appropriate behavior to help set positive examples.

Keeping the Teaching Objective Alive in the Classroom: An Area to Clean

Materials Needed

- Child-sized broom and dustpan
- Kitchen towel(s)
- Sponge(s)
- Dishpan

What to Do

1. To teach the children how to sweep, put a small pile of shredded newspaper on the floor. Show the children how to sweep it onto the dustpan. You might want to let them sweep crumbs from the eating area after snack time.

2. To teach them how to wash and dry, let them wash toy dishes, serving utensils, or paintbrushes.

Teaching Repentance

- Repentance and forgiveness go together. This activity can symbolize both. First, when one repents and confesses, one is often said to "come clean." Tell the children when they confess that they have done something wrong and apologize, the sin is cleaned off their souls. Just as the broom sweeps the mess from the floor, making confession asks Jesus to clean the wrongdoing from the hearts.

- The Bible tells us that if we confess our sins, God is faithful and just; He will forgive us. Help your children understand that when they apologize to God for something, God removes the sin from their souls and forgives them. Just as the water washes the food off the dishes, God washes our souls clean.

- Simon probably cleaned his house before Jesus arrived. Use this activity to help your children role-play the Bible story. Guide the children with appropriate suggestions and questions to be sure they understand the story.

Offering Forgiveness: A Circle-Time Game to Teach Repentance and Forgiveness

Materials Needed

- Small, gift-wrapped box
- Small chair

What to Do

1. Have the children sit in a circle.

2. Select one person to sit in the chair, facing away from the group. Set the gift box behind the chair.

3. Choose someone to take the gift box and return to her seat, hiding the box behind her.

4. The child seated in the chair guesses who has the box. If the guess is correct, the one with the box should say, "I'm sorry, I took your box. Please forgive me." The child seated in the chair should practice forgiveness, saying, "I

forgive you, and Jesus does too." The box is returned. The child who took the box now sits in the guessing chair.

5. If the child guesses incorrectly, allow two more guesses. If she still has not guessed correctly, have the child who took the box come forward and confess.

6. Repeat the process until everyone has a chance to sit in the guessing chair. Remember, it is okay if a child prefers to watch rather than participate in this activity. Learning can happen during observation as well.

Teaching Repentance

- Use this Circle-Time Game to teach children confession, making sure the confession contains these elements: a statement of repentance ("I'm sorry."), a brief explanation of the wrongdoing ("I took your box."), and a request for forgiveness ("Please forgive me.")

- Explain that the box looks like a gift because forgiveness is a gift from God. Tell them that whenever they see a gift, it can remind them that God has given them an even greater gift, forgiveness.

Washing Away Our Sins: An Art Project to Teach Forgiveness

Materials Needed

- Washable markers
- Construction paper
- Clothesline
- Clothespins or masking tape
- Plant misting bottle
- Water
- Newspapers

What to Do

1. Set up for this art project as normal. Put the washable markers and the construction paper on the art table. This project will only work with washable markers.

2. Hang the clothesline at the children's height. Spread newspapers underneath. Fill the misting bottle with water.

3. Encourage each child to draw a picture or design with the washable markers. When finished, help him hang it on the clothesline, using either the clothespins or masking tape.

4. Demonstrate how to mist the picture with water. Monitor this activity as children tend to "over water" their picture.

Teaching Repentance

- When the picture gets wet, it radically changes. So it is with Jesus; He changes our lives. Encourage your children to think about how wonderful it is that God sent His Son to be our Savior.

- As the children spray the water, remind them that Jesus washes away their sins. Jesus will forgive them and wash them clean.

- Ask your children if they have a sin in their life that needs to be washed away. Use specific examples to help them think of any wrong they might have done: hit their sibling, disobeyed their parents, said an unkind word. If a child shares a wrongdoing, help say a prayer of repentence, asking for forgiveness. Do not pressure those who cannot think of examples.

Forgiveness Sort: A Center Activity to Teach Repentance

Materials Needed

- Copies of the Forgiveness Sorting Squares (pages 67–68)

- Scissors
- 2 sheets of heavy white paper
- Glue
- Red and blue markers
- Three small baskets
- Red ribbon
- Blue ribbon

What to Do

1. Make copies of the Forgiveness Sorting Squares (pages 67–68)

2. Glue all the Forgiveness Sorting Squares to heavy white paper. When dry, cut along the solid lines. On the backs of the squares showing scenes that need forgiveness, draw a cross with a blue marker. On the backs of those with scenes that do not need forgiveness, draw a heart with the red marker. Laminate the squares, if possible.

3. Tie the red ribbon on one basket and the blue ribbon on the second basket. Put the sorting squares into the third basket.

4. Introduce this activity as you would any new learning center activity. Show the children how to sort the squares into the "Needs Forgiveness" basket (red ribbon) or the "Doesn't Need Forgiveness" basket (blue ribbon).

5. When they have finished sorting, show how to self-check the work using the colored shape on the back of each square.

Teaching Repentance

- Talk to your children about the various pictures. Help them identify the sinful actions, encouraging them to think of appropriate ways to ask for forgiveness in each situation.

- Show scenes from the Bible story. Help the children identify those scenes. Ask them to tell you what is happening. Guide their retelling of the story through questions and prompts.

- A child may volunteer that she has committed one of the wrongful acts shown. If so, ask how she asked for forgiveness. If she has not yet repented, encourage her to do so. Seeking forgiveness is important in a Christian's faith life.

Making A-mends: A Circle-Time Game to Teach Repentance

Materials Needed

- Small plastic bowls, one for each pair of children

- Scissors

- Small paper or plastic bags, one for each bowl

- Masking tape

What to Do

1. Before Circle Time, cut each plastic bowl into three or four pieces. Put each bowl in a separate paper or plastic bag.

2. During Circle Time, help the children chose partners. Give each pair a bag and about 12" of masking tape.

3. Tell your children to open their bag and take out the pieces of the broken bowl. Encourage them to work together to mend the bowl with the masking tape.

4. When all the bowls are repaired, ask the children how it felt to find the broken bowl. How did they feel once the bowl was fixed?

Teaching Repentance

- When a person does something wrong, that person often feels bad inside. Compare this bad feeling with how the children felt when they received a broken bowl.

- Mending the bowls is like saying "I'm sorry." It is a way of making something broken whole again.

- This game builds on the lessons learned and values practiced from the previous three units. First, the children must work patiently, just as Abraham and Sarah worked patiently to prepare food for their guests. Second, they must use kind words, just as Ruth used kind words with Naomi. Finally, the children must work together to solve a problem, just like Jonathan and David. If you discover a pair struggling in one of these areas, remind them of the Bible stories and the value learned.

Swinging the Verse: A Circle-Time Game to Teach the Bible Memory Verse

Materials Needed

- Copy of the Bible memory verse (page 64)

- Jump rope

What to Do

1. During Circle Time, hold up the copy of the Bible memory verse. Say it with the children several times, pointing to each word.

2. Pick two children to swing the jump rope. Show them how to swing it slowly and evenly, not too far above the ground.

3. Have the other children line up facing the swinging jump rope. Tell them to jump over it one at a time, chanting the verse as they do.

4. Switch rope swingers. Repeat the process until everyone knows the verse.

Teaching Repentance

- In this game, children have an opportunity to put motion with the Bible memory verse. This active learning will help them memorize the Scripture.

- This game also provides opportunities for practicing repentance and forgiveness. If the rope is swung too high, encourage the jumpers to practice forgiveness. When a jumper gets tangled up in the rope, model a statement of forgiveness for the swingers to say.

- Jumping over a swinging rope can be hard for young children. Remind them to be patient and persevere, just as Abraham and Sarah did. Encourage those watching to cheer for the jumpers, using kind words like Ruth. Remind them to take turns and be friendly with each other, just like David and Jonathan.

A Special Gift: An Art Project to Teach the Bible Memory Verse

Materials Needed

- Copies of Jesus' Forgiveness Package (page 69), at least one per child
- Wrapping paper
- Scissors, child-sized and adult-sized
- Glue
- Tape

What to Do

1. Before class, cut the wrapping paper into small squares, about 1" × 1".

2. Arrange materials for this art project, putting the copies, wrapping paper squares, scissors, glue, and tape on the art table.

3. Show the children how to cut out the Forgiveness Package by cutting on the solid lines only. If you have younger children, you may need to help them with this step (or you may need to pre-cut the packages).

4. Have the children glue the squares of gift wrap on the back of the Forgiveness Packages. Encourage them to completely cover the package.

5. When the packages are dry, show the children how to fold on the dotted lines to cover the Bible memory verse. Give them a small piece of tape to keep their package closed.

Teaching Repentance

- Read the Bible memory verse individually to the children as you work on this project. Ask them about other great gifts they have been given. Remind them that Jesus and His forgiveness are the greatest gifts ever given.

- Ask the children if someone in their life has recently done something to upset them. If so, ask if the offender has been forgiven. If not, encourage the child to forgive because Christ forgives. Be sure to follow up on this discussion, reinforcing that forgiveness and repentance are important in a Christian's faith life.

- Waiting for the glue to dry is a natural opportunity to encourage the children to practice patience. Sharing the art materials, working space, and your attention also provides openings for you to remind the children to be like Ruth, and David and Jonathan—friendly and kind in their actions and deeds!

Telling the Story

To tell the story for this unit, first read the account in Luke 7:36–50. Make a copy of the puzzle on page 65 on poster board or other heavy paper. Color the puzzle, cut out the pieces, and put them in a small decorated box or container. Read aloud the words in bold print, and follow the actions in italics.

Pass this box around the circle while I tell the story. Whenever I say Jesus or Mary, the person holding the box should take off the cover, remove a puzzle piece, and start building our puzzle. At the end of the story, we will see the whole puzzle put together. Ready?

Once there was a man named Simon. He wanted to have someone very important come to his house for dinner. One day, Simon invited Jesus to have dinner with him. *Help the child who is holding the box remove a puzzle piece and put it in the center of the circle.* **Jesus and all His disciples went to Simon's house.** *Help a child remove a puzzle piece and add it to the puzzle.* **When Jesus was alive, they did not sit on chairs at a table like we do.** *Add another piece.* **Instead, the table was very low to the ground and people sat on the floor. So, when Jesus came to Simon's house, He sat on the floor next to the table and ate dinner.** *Add another piece.*

Mary was a woman who had done some things that were wrong. She was very sorry for her sins. *Add another piece.* **When she heard that Jesus was eating at Simon's house, she brought a jar of perfume to the house.** *Add another piece.* **When Mary saw Jesus, she began to cry and washed His feet with her tears.** *Add two pieces.* **Then she wiped His feet with her hair, kissed them, and poured perfume on them. "I'm sorry,"
she said, over and over again.**

When Simon saw this, he thought that Jesus would not want her to touch Him because Mary had done many bad things in her life. *Add two pieces.*

Jesus looked at Simon and He knew what Simon had been thinking. *Add another piece.* **Jesus said, "Simon, I want to tell you a story."** *Add another piece.* **Two men owed money to a certain moneylender. One owed him five hundred pieces of money, and the other man owed him only fifty pieces of money. Neither of them had enough money to pay him back, so the moneylender said it was OK. They didn't have to pay him back. Now which of them will love him more?"**

Simon thought for a moment and then answered, "I suppose the one who owed the most money." "Yes," said Jesus. "You are right." *Add another piece.*

Then Jesus said to Simon, "When I came into your house, My feet were very dirty from walking on the dusty road all day. *Add another piece.* **You did not give Me any water to wash My feet. Do you see this woman? She wet My feet with her tears and wiped them with her hair. She has poured perfume on My feet. She has repented and said she is sorry for the bad things she has done."**

Then Jesus said to Mary, "Your sins are forgiven. Your faith has saved you. Go in peace." *Finish the puzzle by adding the remaining pieces.*

When the puzzle is completed, you can tell the story again, without the puzzle activity. This time, let the children focus on the story rather than the puzzle.

Bible Memory Verse

Your sins are forgiven.

Mark 2:5 (NIV)

Puzzle

Forgiveness Sorting Squares, page 1

Forgiveness Sorting Squares, page 2

Jesus' Forgiveness Package

Your sins
are forgiven.

Mark 2:5 (NIV)

Dear Parent(s),

"I'm sorry." Preschoolers seem to get into lots of trouble. You chastise your child and the same transgression is still repeated over and over again. When caught doing something wrong, a child cries and begs to have another chance, to avoid the consequence, and to be forgiven. Jesus gave His life on the cross to pay for our sins, and, like our own children, we go to our heavenly Father with our transgressions and receive forgiveness over and over again. This month, our class will learn how Mary asked for and received forgiveness.

The lessons of Mary and forgiveness shouldn't stop at the classroom door. I invite you to share these lessons with your child at home by reading the story of Mary from a preschool Bible, trying the activities provided in this letter, and teaching this Bible memory verse.

Your sins are forgiven. *Mark 2:5*

Learning to ask for, accept, and offer forgiveness takes time and practice. You can help your child learn about forgiveness by first knowing how children understand forgiveness at different ages.

How Children Learn about Forgiveness

Age 3: A 3-year-old will say the words, "I'm sorry," when she knows she has broken a rule or hurt a friend. Sometimes she will say the words without prompting from an adult, but more often she will need a gentle reminder. At 3, they are just beginning to recognize the way someone else might feel and the impact of their actions on others. You can help your child understand apologies and forgiveness by setting a good example. When you lose your temper or fail to keep a promise, remember to say "I'm sorry." When she tells you that she made a mistake and is sorry, remember to say, "I forgive you." Tell her that Jesus loves her with all her faults and failings, and you do too. Continue to teach through your good example that asking for forgiveness is a rewarding experience.

Age 4: 4-year-olds are becoming aware of "good" and "bad." They may become more spontaneous in prayer, asking God to help them be good. Help them understand the difference between accidental and intentional wrongs. "You didn't mean to break the lamp. The ball accidentally hit the lamp. But you chose to break our rule—no ball bouncing in the house." Establish a few important rules, explain the reasons for these rules, set forth consequences for breaking the rules, and remain calm and matter-of-fact when enforcing them. 4-year-olds can begin to connect the "badness" of breaking a rule with the bad feelings connected to failure and the good feelings connected to apologies and forgiveness.

Age 5: At 5, children can better understand the concepts of confession, "I did something wrong and I'm sorry"; and absolution, "You have forgiven me and we will start again fresh." Use every opportunity to point out these components in daily encounters with friends, family members, Bible and storybook characters, and TV presentations. When you must point out a child's transgression, do it as quietly and privately as possible. It is easier to apologize and receive forgiveness when not embarrassed by the presence of others.

Parent's Prayer

Heavenly Father, You sent Your only Son to die on the cross to pay for my sins, and I come to you many times each day, penitent and asking for forgiveness. Help me to accept my child's mistakes with the same loving forgiveness and guidance that You give to me. In Jesus' name I pray. Amen.

Together in Christ,

Family Activities

Forgiveness Pockets: A Cooking Adventure

Ingredients

- Refrigerator biscuits
- A can of pie filling, any flavor
- Cookie sheet, ungreased
- Fork

What to Do

1. Flatten each biscuit slightly.
2. Put half of the flattened biscuits on the ungreased cookie sheet.
3. Help your child put a heaping spoonful of pie filling in the center of each flattened biscuit. Cover each with one of the remaining biscuits.
4. Show your child how to use the fork to seal the edges, pressing down firmly with the tines.
5. Bake the Forgiveness Pockets at 375 degrees for 10 minutes, or until brown. Cool and enjoy!

Teaching Repentance

- As you share the Forgiveness Pockets with your child, comment on how sweet they are. Remind your child that forgiveness is just as sweet. To be forgiven sweetens the soul; to forgive someone else sweetens the relationship.

- Should a mishap happen with the cooking supplies, encourage your child to ask for forgiveness. Help choose the right words to express repentance.

- Help your child retell the story by asking these questions: Who cooked a meal for Jesus? (Simon the Pharisee) Who poured perfume on Jesus' feet? (Mary) What did Jesus say to her? ("Your sins are forgiven.") What did Simon think? ("Jesus should know that she is a sinner. He should not let her near Him.")

Snow White Hearts: An Art Project

Materials Needed

- 2 cups of powdered laundry soap (not detergent)
- ½ cup water
- Electric mixer
- Mixing bowl
- Old shower curtain or other suitable covering for the work surface

What to Do

1. Pour the powdered laundry soap into a mixing bowl.
2. Let your child add the water.
3. Use the electric mixer to whip the mixture until it resembles dough.
4. Scoop the mixture onto the old shower curtain. Help your child form it into a variety of shapes. Be sure to form at least one heart. Put decorations such as buttons, yarn, feathers, and sequins into the shapes.
5. When you are done molding, let the shapes dry for several hours.

Teaching Repentance

- As the hearts dry, notice that the grayish tinge disappears and the shapes become bright white. Explain to your child that the dark color reminds us of our sin. However, when we say, "I'm sorry," and receive forgiveness, our hearts become clean and white again.

- Ask your child if she has a sin in her life that needs to be washed away. Use specific examples to help her think of anything wrong she might have done: hit a sibling, disobeyed a parent, said an unkind word, etc. Help her say a prayer repenting and asking for forgiveness. If your child does not offer an example, do not pressure her. Remind her the soap washed away the dirt and that God promised to wash away our sins.

- Help your child retell the story by asking questions such as: What did Mary say to Jesus? ("I'm sorry. Please forgive me.") What did Jesus say? ("Yes, I will forgive you. Your heart has been made clean.")

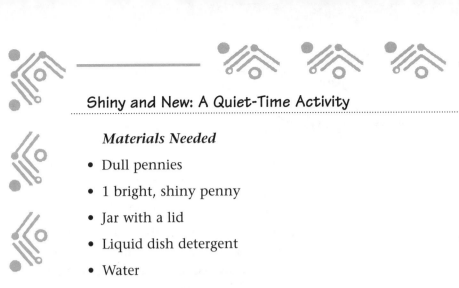

Shiny and New: A Quiet-Time Activity

Materials Needed

- Dull pennies
- 1 bright, shiny penny
- Jar with a lid
- Liquid dish detergent
- Water
- ½ cup white vinegar
- 3 tablespoons salt

What to Do

1. Look at the pennies with your child. Tell him whose face is on the front, and see what other pictures and words are on the penny.

2. Show your child that many of the pennies are dull, but one of them is shiny. Challenge your child to try and make the dull pennies shiny. Together, put some water and a little detergent in the jar. Add some of the dull pennies, and screw the lid on the jar. Shake the jar well. Open the jar and drain off the water. Check your pennies. Are they shiny or just wet?

3. Rinse the jar clean. Let your child pour the white vinegar into the jar. Pour in the salt. Add some of the dull pennies. Screw the lid on the jar and shake the jar well. Open the jar and drain off the special cleaning solution. Are the pennies shiny now? Or are they still just wet? Rinse the pennies.

Teaching Repentance

- Did ordinary soap and water clean the pennies? No! It took a special cleaning solution to do that. Explain to your child that just ignoring a wrong action or trying to act "extra nice" will not make it "all better." Instead, she needs to use a special cleaning solution, saying, "I'm sorry" and asking for forgiveness.

- Link this activity to the story by asking these questions: Who had dirty feet? (Jesus) Who made them clean? (Mary) What special cleaning solution did she use? (Tears and perfumed oil) Did Jesus forgive her and clean her heart? (Yes) What was His special cleaning solution? (God's forgiveness)

Other Simple Ideas

1. Model how to say, "I'm sorry," to your children if you have failed them in any way. Let them hear you seeking forgiveness from God in prayer.

Say Thank You!

One Man Remembers

Bible Memory Verse

Always giving thanks to God the Father for everything. *Ephesians 5:20*

Teacher's Prayer

Heavenly Father, I practice good manners, know what it means to be polite, and always say thank you when someone gives me a gift. But there is more to being thankful than merely saying these words. Help me to "give thanks in all circumstances" (1 Thessalonians 5:18). Help me be content with the blessings You have given me, refrain from complaints, and serve others as a way of showing appreciation for Your many gifts. Let my words and actions of appreciation flow freely toward You and the children so they may learn thankfulness through me. In Jesus' name I pray. Amen.

Teaching Objective: Thankfulness

To help children learn to be thankful just as one of the ten lepers thanked Jesus for making him well.

Through God's Word and the power of the Holy Spirit, by the end of this unit, the children should be able to:

1. Tell the basic story of Jesus and the 10 Lepers.

2. Repeat the Bible memory verse.

3. Comprehend the teaching objective *thankfulness.*

4. Show an increased ability to be thankful.

5. Say thank you more frequently.

Learning to be thankful takes time and practice. In order to be thankful and express thanks, a child needs to learn words to express thanks, learn when to use these words of thanks, and finally to truly feel thankful. You can help the children learn thankfulness by recognizing and remembering how children express thanks at different ages.

How Children Learn Thankfulness

Age 3: Though 3-year-olds are not bad-mannered or unappreciative, their behavior often makes them appear that way to adults. They have not had enough practice repeating thank you in response to all the situations in which they should express gratitude. At 3, they do not understand another person's feelings or perspective. They do not see the need to express their appreciation in response to a gift or service received. 3-year-olds can best learn thankfulness by hearing you express your thanks for things they have done or offered. Your classroom prayers might include the phrase, "Thank You, Lord, for the children, a special gift from You." Hugs, high-five gestures, and a desire to be close to you are also expressions of the thankfulness of children. Remember to appreciate their special expressions of thanks.

Age 4: Many 4-year-olds are beginning to enjoy art projects for the end product as well as the experiential process. You can encourage them to use these projects as thank-you letters for gifts, efforts, and kindnesses given to them. This provides a way to express their appreciation through thoughtfulness, effort, and a tangible gift. While 3-year-olds concentrated on repeating the words thank you at appropriate times, 4-year-olds can be prompted to expand their thanks by saying, "Thank you for giving me a turn"; "Thank you for inviting me to play"; "Thank you for the sweater." It helps to prompt children by asking questions that will not embarrass them. "Wasn't it nice that Ben shared the truck with you?" "Did you enjoy your visit to the pumpkin farm?" or "What did Sarah give you?" are better reminders than the admonitions, "What do you say?" or "Did you say thank you?"

Age 5: At 5, children are beginning to understand that it takes effort and desire to do things for them or provide them with a gift. Empathy—the capacity to put oneself in another's place—is beginning to develop. While it could not be rushed or understood earlier, 5-year-olds are capable of feeling more thankfulness and gratitude. The ability to empathize, plus the 5-year-old's desire to please and cooperate, creates the perfect opportunity to emphasize expressions of thanksgiving through words, actions, and prayers. Practice over the years of saying the words thank you can now inspire the expression of appreciation through a grateful spirit.

Teaching Activities

A Banner of Thanks: Keeping the Theme Alive in the Classroom

Materials Needed

- Banner/mural paper
- Pictures cut from magazines and catalogs
- Assorted objects from nature: flowers, leaves, twigs, etc.
- Anything else that represents things for which the children are thankful
- Construction paper
- Crayons
- Glue
- Scissors, child-sized
- Marker

What to Do

1. Before school starts, lay the banner/mural paper on the art table. Set the collage materials around it. Put the scissors and glue nearby.

2. Use the marker to write "Things We Are Thankful For" or the Bible memory verse across the top of the banner.

3. As the children approach the table, encourage them to select pictures, nature objects, or other things to glue on the banner.

4. Encourage them to use the construction paper and crayons to draw pictures of things they are thankful for that are not represented in the collection of collage items. Help them cut out these pictures.

5. When the glue is dry, hang the banner in a prominent place.

Teaching Thankfulness

- This project can remain in progress for one day, one week, or one month.

- Suggest that the children draw a picture of Jesus or heaven as they imagine it to look. Remind them that God's love, Jesus' care, and eternal life are all things to be thankful for. Most important, tell them that Jesus is happy to hear their words of thanks, just like friends and family appreciate hearing the words "thank you."

- Wonder, with the children, what kind of things the thankful leper might have glued onto a banner. Would they be different from the things they glued on their own banner?

Sewing Thanks: Decorating the Bible Memory Verse

Materials Needed

- Bible memory verse (page 81)
- Poster board or cardboard (flattened cereal boxes work well) 4 ¼" × 5 ½", one piece per child
- Star stickers, one per child
- Hole punch
- Yarn
- Scissors
- Masking tape

What to Do

1. Make copies of the Bible memory verse, one for each child.

2. Cut the copies to fit the cardboard and glue a Bible memory verse onto each piece. The children may be able to help with this step.

3. Punch ten holes around the edge of each of the Bible memory verses.

4. Cut pieces of yarn long enough to "sew" through all the holes. Cut one piece of yarn per Bible memory verse.

5. Tape one end of the yarn to the back of each card.

6. Fold masking tape around the other end of the yarn so it can function as a simple needle.

7. When the children arrive, have them place a star sticker near one of the punched-out holes. Show them how to use the taped end of the yarn to sew in and out of the holes, all around the edge of the cardboard. The cards will probably end up with a crisscross pattern when completed.

Teaching Thankfulness

- The hole with the star sticker represents the thankful leper who returned to Jesus. Remind the children that though ten were healed, only one was thankful. How do they think Jesus felt when the leper said thank you? Bright and shiny, like the star stickers.

- Read the Bible memory verse individually to the children. Help them think of ten things for which they might thank their parents, friends, or siblings. Encourage them to say those thank you's. Be sure to follow up with the children. In so doing, you will reinforce the importance of showing gratitude.

Saying Thanks: A Circle-Time Game to Teach Thankfulness

Materials Needed

- Cookies (or other snack), at least one per child
- Plate
- Napkins, one per child
- Hungry kids

What to Do

1. Seat the children in a circle and have one child hand out the napkins. Be sure to say thank you to your hard worker!

2. Take the plate of cookies (or other snack) and walk around the inside of the circle. Offer the plate to a child, and tell him to take a cookie and put it on his napkin.

3. After the cookie is placed on the child's napkin, pause briefly to allow the child to spontaneously say thank you. If he forgets, whisper a reminder to him. After he says thank you, ask him to pass the plate to another child.

4. Each child should have a turn to take a cookie, say thank you, and pass the plate.

Teaching Thankfulness

- After all the children have a cookie, say a prayer of thanks to God. Remember to thank God for the cookies, for sweet treats, for grateful children, and most of all, for His Son, Jesus Christ.

- While eating the cookies, talk about other ways to say thank you. If you know how to say thank you in a foreign language, teach the children. You might want to teach them the American Sign Language sign for thank you: touch the fingertips of one hand to your chin and move outward and down.

- This activity builds on the previous four units in this book. Thank the children who are waiting patiently; compliment them for acting like Abraham and Sarah. Admire those children who use kind words; praise them for acting like Ruth. Acknowledge those children who share willingly; thank them for acting like good friends David and Jonathan. Is there a mishap? Remind those involved of the need to ask for and grant forgiveness; help them remember Mary, who was forgiven.

A Bright Word: An Art Project to Teach Thankfulness

Materials Needed

- Colored chalk (bright colors work best)
- Thick, black tempera paint
- Jar lid or other shallow container
- White paper
- Newspapers

What to Do

1. Set up for this activity as you would other art projects, covering the table with newspaper. Put the white paper on the table. Pour a small amount of the thick black tempera paint into the jar lid. The container needs to be shallow to limit the depth of the paint.

2. Show the children how to dip one end of the chalk into the thick tempera paint.

3. Let them draw with the paint-dipped chalk onto the white paper. The lines will show the bright color of the chalk between black outlines.

4. Suggest they try a variety of strokes: zigzags, spirals, dots, curves, letters, numbers, verticals, horizontals, etc.

5. Tell them to dip the chalk again when necessary.

Teaching Thankfulness

- How is saying thank you like this art technique? A sincere thank you can brighten someone's day. No matter what you look like on the outside, showing gratitude reveals you are bright and cheery on the inside. The chalk can draw many different kinds of lines, and there are many different ways to express appreciation. Can you and the children think of other similarities?

- After the thankful leper was healed, he experienced new freedoms: the freedom to enter the house of worship, to mingle with healthy people, to touch others. Let the children experience a similar freedom by allowing them to enjoy the process of this art project without the pressure to produce a recognizable product. Focus your thanks on their efforts, not their finished pictures.

- Should you overhear the children thanking each other during this project, quietly recognize their efforts, helping them feel bright and cheery on the inside.

One Returns: A Circle-Time Game to Teach the Story

Materials Needed

- 10 pieces of paper
- Marker
- Masking tape

What to Do

1. Number the papers from one to ten.

2. Use the masking tape to tape them sequentially in a line on the floor. Use the tape to mark an "X" on the floor as a starting point, about 12″ from the paper number 1.

3. Select a child to be the thankful leper and stand on the starting point. Choose another child to be the priest. Send that child to stand on a paper of another number you choose, 6 for example.

4. Tell the thankful leper, "Go! Show yourself to the priest by walking backward (or jumping or skipping or crawling like a snake, etc.) to the number 6." Pause while the thankful leper follows directions.

5. Have the thankful child return to the starting point and gently prompt him to say thank you. The child who was the priest now becomes the thankful leper. Choose a new priest, and repeat the process until everyone has a turn.

Teaching Thankfulness

- How many of the children spontaneously said thank you? Hopefully, more than 10 percent!

- Encourage your thankful lepers to say thank you in as many ways as possible. Help them think of different thankful phrases as well as a variety of ways to move during the game.

- How hard it is to wait to be healed! Be sure to acknowledge those children patiently waiting for their turn. Model various ways to say thank you.

Thankful Talk: A Center Activity to Teach Thankfulness

Materials Needed

- 2 Thankful Talk Reproducible pages (page 83)
- Scissors
- Construction paper, 2 different colors
- Glue
- 2 paper clips
- Small basket

What to Do

1. Make two copies of the Thankful Talk Reproducible pages. Cut the cards apart on the solid lines.

2. Glue one set of cards to one color of construction paper, leaving a ¼″ border on all sides. Glue the other set of cards to the second color construction paper. Paper clip each set together. Place in the small basket.

3. Follow your standard classroom procedure to introduce this new center activity.

4. Explain that this game is played in pairs. Each child will have one set of cards. Each card will have an identical match in the other set.

5. Have the first child describe the picture on one card and explain why someone would be thankful for the activity pic-

tured. The other child then selects the card that matches the description. Show the card selected to the first child. If they match, lay them aside. If not, the second child should try again.

6. Repeat until all the cards have been matched.

Teaching Thankfulness

• Listen carefully as the children describe why they might be grateful for the pictured activity. Be sure to reward creative thoughts!

• Listen as the children play the game. Are they being polite? Are they using kind words? Do you hear thank you being said? If so, then rejoice that the value for this lesson is being incorporated into everyday activities. If not, urge the children to be more like the thankful leper and use kind words, polite behaviors, and thankful actions.

• Preschoolers love repetition. Use this activity to repeat suggestions for teaching thankfulness made in other activities. Thanks! Your perseverance is appreciated!

Walking to the Priests: A Circle-Time Game to Teach the Bible Memory Verse

Materials Needed

• 10 pieces of paper
• Masking tape
• A copy of the Bible memory verse (page 81)

What to Do

1. Tape the ten pieces of paper to the floor in a circle.

2. Choose ten children. Have each one stand on a piece of paper. Explain that

as they step onto each piece of paper, the class will say one word of the Bible memory verse, including the reference.

3. Repeat until the children have the verse memorized. Switch children as needed.

Teaching Thankfulness

• Pause in your activity to retell the story. Ask the children how many lepers came to Jesus? (Ten) Where did they walk? (To the priests) How many came back to Jesus? (One) What did the one leper say? (Thank You!)

• Acknowledge the children's effort to learn this verse. It is hard to memorize Scripture; applaud their attempts!

• What does "everything" mean? Ask the children what kind of things they are thankful for. List things glued onto the banner, the activities pictured on the Thankful Talk cards, art projects, cookies and other snacks, healthy bodies, and more.

Thankful Streamers: A Craft Project to Teach the Bible Memory Verse

Materials Needed

• Paper plates, one per child
• Copies of the Thankful Streamer Bible memory verse (page 84), one per child
• Scissors
• Glue
• Crepe paper
• Stapler and staples
• Your choice of decorative stickers, stamps, crayons, markers, glue, and glitter

What to Do

1. Cut each paper plate in half. Cut a semi-

circle out of each plate to form a handle (see diagram).

2. Cut out the copies of the Thankful Streamer Bible memory verse. Have the children do this if their skill with scissors is up to the challenge.

3. Cut the crepe paper into streamers about 12–15" in length, six per child.

4. Put the glue, crepe paper streamers, stapler, staples, and your choice of decorations on the art table.

5. Help the children glue the Bible memory verse onto their plates. Let them decorate their plates.

6. Help them staple the crepe paper streamers to the plates, three per plate (see diagram).

7. Go outside and run wild with the thankful streamers.

Telling the Story

To tell the story for this unit, review the story as based on Luke 17:11–19. You will need to collect photos of each child in the class. (A note for the parents to send nonreturnable photos is included in the Parent's Letter.) Carefully cut around the faces of each child. Make copies of the Story Bodies,

found on page 82, and cut them out. Let the children color the clothes and glue the photo of their own face onto their story body. If there are fewer than 10 children in your class, add more photo faces. You might choose to include the teachers' faces or faces cut from magazines. You will also need a felt board. Add a loop of masking tape to the back of each story body so they will stick to the felt board. Read the text written in bold print and follow the directions written in italics.

Jesus was walking to Jerusalem. *Put the figure of Jesus on the felt board.* **On His way, He met ten men.** *Add the ten story bodies.* **The ten men had leprosy, a disease that made their skin turn white and bumpy. People who had leprosy were not allowed to live with healthy people. They stood at a distance and called out in loud voices, "Jesus, Master, have pity on us!"**

When Jesus saw them He said, "Go, show yourselves to the priests." As they ran to find the priests, they were healed from leprosy. *Take down all of the leper figures.*

One of them, *put one of the lepers back on the felt board,* **saw that he was healed and came back. He threw himself at Jesus' feet. The man said, "Thank You, Jesus! Thank You for making me well again! Thank You for what you have done! Thank You!"**

Jesus asked, "Didn't I heal all ten men? Where are the other nine? Why didn't they come back to say thank you?"

Then Jesus said to the man, "Get up and go. Your faith has made you well." *Remove both men from the felt board.*

Repeat this story until all of the children have a chance to be the man who came back to say thank you. When finished, put the felt board and figures where the children can use them to reenact the story during free time.

Bible Memory Verse

Always giving thanks to God the Father for everything.

Ephesians 5:20 (NIV)

Story Bodies

Teacher's Note: Make two copies of this page to make 10 story bodies. You will have one extra Jesus.

Thankful Talk

Thankful Streamer Bible Memory Verse

Always giving thanks to God the Father for everything.

Ephesians 5:20 (NIV)

Always giving thanks to God the Father for everything.

Ephesians 5:20 (NIV)

Always giving thanks to God the Father for everything.

Ephesians 5:20 (NIV)

Dear Parent(s),

Remember to say thank you.

This month, our class will learn about the ten lepers who were healed by Jesus. Only one returned to say thank you. We will emphasize saying the words thank you, as well as ways to show appreciation, through service, to others. **Please send a photograph of your child's face for use in our classroom thankfulness project. A wallet-size photo will be fine. Photos are needed by _____ and will not be returned.**

The lesson of the ten lepers should not end at the classroom door. I invite you to share this lesson with your child at home by reading the story of Jesus and the ten lepers from a preschool Bible, trying the activities provided in this letter, and teaching this Bible memory verse.

Always giving thanks to God the Father for everything. *Ephesians 5:20*

Learning to be thankful takes time and practice. In order to be thankful and express thanks, a child needs to learn words that express thanks, learn when to use these words of thanks, and finally to truly feel thankful. You can help your child learn thankfulness by understanding how children express thanks at different ages.

How Children Learn Thankfulness

Age 3: Though 3-year-olds are not bad-mannered or unappreciative, their behavior often makes them appear that way to adults. They have not had enough practice repeating the words thank you in response to all the situations in which they should express gratitude. At 3, they do not understand another person's feelings or perspective. They do not see the need to express their appreciation in response to a gift or service received. 3-year-olds can best learn thankfulness by hearing you express your thanks for things they have done or offered. Your prayers might include the phrase, "Thank You, Lord, for my child, a special gift from You." Hugs, high-five gestures, and a desire to be close to you are also expressions of the thankfulness of children. Remember to appreciate their special expressions of thanks.

Age 4: Many 4-year-olds are beginning to enjoy art projects for the end product as well as the experiential process. You can encourage them to use these projects as thank-you letters for gifts, efforts, and kindnesses given to them. This provides a way to express their appreciation through thoughtfulness, effort, and a tangible gift. While 3-year-olds concentrated on repeating the words thank you at appropriate times, 4-year-olds can be prompted to expand their thanks by saying, "Thank you for giving me a turn"; "Thank you for inviting me to play"; "Thank you for the sweater." It helps to prompt children by asking questions that will not embarrass them. "Wasn't it nice that Ben shared the truck with you?" "Did you enjoy your visit to the pumpkin farm?" or "What did Sarah give you?" are better reminders than the admonitions, "What do you say?" or "Did you say thank you?"

Age 5: At 5, children are beginning to understand that it takes effort and desire to do things for them or provide them with a gift. Empathy—the capacity to put oneself in another's place—is beginning to develop. While it could not be rushed or understood earlier, 5-year-olds are capable of feeling more thankfulness and gratitude. The ability to empathize, plus the 5-year-old's desire to please and cooperate, creates the perfect opportunity to emphasize expressions of thanksgiving through words, actions, and prayers. Practice over the years of saying the words thank you can now inspire the expression of appreciation through a grateful spirit.

Parent's Prayer

Heavenly Father, I practice good manners, know what it means to be polite, and always say thank you when someone gives me a gift. But there is more to being thankful than merely saying these words. Help me to "give thanks in all circumstances" (1 Thessalonians 5:18), be content with the blessings You have given me, refrain from complaints, and serve others as a way to show appreciation for Your many gifts. Let my words and actions of appreciation flow freely toward You and my child. In Jesus' name I pray. Amen.

Together in Christ,

Family Activities

Favorite Foods: A Cooking Adventure

Ingredients

• Your child's favorite food, either snack or meal

What to Do

1. Prepare your child's favorite food. Encourage her to help in the preparation.
2. Sit down to feast upon this delicacy with your child. Pause a moment to say thank you to God for your food. Urge your child to voice his thanks too!
3. Eat!

Teaching Thankfulness

• While enjoying this treat, make a list of all the people who helped make this food: farmers, truckers, grocery store workers, etc. Offer a prayer of thanks to God for all these faithful servants.

• Thank your child for sharing this treat with you. After all, it can be very hard to share a favorite food.

- Did your child thank you for your part in this treat? If not, gently prompt him to do so. If he did express thanks, tell him you appreciate his gratitude.

- Help your child tell the story by asking these questions: How many lepers came to Jesus? (Ten) Could lepers eat with healthy people? (No) Which leper made Jesus happy? (The one who came back and said thank You.)

Thankful Decorations: A Craft Project

Materials Needed

- 1 cup applesauce
- 1 ½ cups (6 oz.) cinnamon
- ⅓ cup white glue
- Bowl
- Rolling pin
- Cookie cutters
- Plastic straw
- Drying rack(s)
- Ribbon

What to Do

1. Mix the applesauce, cinnamon, and glue in a bowl until the mixture forms a ball.

2. Put the dough in the refrigerator for 30 minutes or longer.

3. Sprinkle extra cinnamon on a cutting board to prevent dough from sticking. Roll out the dough to ¼" thick.

4. Cut dough with cookie cutters.

5. Use a plastic straw to poke a hole in the top of each decoration.

6. Put the decorations on the drying rack(s) and let dry for about two days. When the decorations change from dark brown to light brown, they are dry.

7. Tie a piece of ribbon through the hole in each decoration. Now they are ready to be hung. The ornaments will provide a nice fragrance—something to be thankful for.

Teaching Thankfulness

- As you make these ornaments, thank and praise God for each of the senses the decorations stimulate: the wonderful smell of cinnamon, the rough feel of the dough, the pleasing sight of the finished project, and the rewarding sound of a family working together. Do not taste these decorations, you won't be thankful when you taste the glue.

- Be sure to model gratitude as you make these decorations with your child. Say thank you for her help and acknowledge her thankful words.

- Help your child tell the story by asking these questions: Who did the lepers see first? (Jesus) Who did Jesus tell them to go and see? (The priests) How did they feel after they were healed? (Happy, excited, thankful)

Materials Needed

- Completed Thankful Decorations
- An appropriate destination: church, school, fire station, police station, an emergency room (obviously not during a very busy time).

What to Do

1. With your child, select appropriate recipients of these decorations. Try to pick people whose services are vital, but who are often overlooked when it comes to gratitude. Be sure to ask your child for suggestions.

2. Visit the destination, leaving your thanks and ornaments with those faithful servants.

Teaching Thankfulness

- Talk with your child about why you are thankful for the chosen recipient. Do they keep your house safe? Do they heal your body? Do they nurture your soul?

- Encourage your child to say thank you to these public servants, experiencing the joy of expressing gratitude.

- Did the workers say thank you? Were they touched? Did some have tears in their eyes? Point out how powerful an experience this simple act was.

- Help your child retell the story by asking these questions: What did the thankful leper say? (Thank You for healing me.) How many men said thank you? (Only one) How do you think Jesus felt when He was thanked? (Powerfully moved, just like the quiet laborer who received the decoration)

Be Brave!

David Trusts God

Bible Memory Verse

The LORD is my strength and my shield. *Psalm 28:7*

Teacher's Prayer

Heavenly Father, I want these children to trust me to teach and nurture them, yet I often fail to trust in You. David's faith gave him the courage to stand up to a giant problem. Lord, please give me the courage to trust You as I face life's problems. Help me show my faith and courage to the children so they will also learn to stand up to their fears and trust Your protective arms around them. In Jesus' name I pray. Amen.

Teaching Objective: Courage

To help children learn to trust in the Lord, face their fears, and be brave just as David trusted God and faced the fearsome Goliath.

Through God's Word and the power of the Holy Spirit, by the end of this unit, the children should be able to:

1. Tell the basic story of David and Goliath.
2. Repeat the Bible memory verse.
3. Comprehend the teaching objective *bravery*.
4. Show an increased ability to be brave.
5. Distinguish between big and little.

Learning to have courage and face fears takes time and practice. In order to have courage, a child must first learn to trust. Trust in parents, self, teachers, and the Lord. You can help the children learn to have courage by building a foundation of trust and recognizing and remembering how children learn courage at different ages.

How Children Learn to Have Courage

Age 3: Fear of the dark, fear of monsters, fear of new situations, fear of animals—3-year-olds are beginning to develop rich fantasy lives and are starting to realize the world can be a dangerous and scary place. At 3, a child needs to have those fears accepted and respected. Time is needed to adjust to scary situations. The child's trust will grow as you keep promises, provide protection, encourage trying new things, and generously praise efforts. This is a good time to protect the child from fears, allow room to express fears, and be present to provide support in frightening situations. It is not a good idea to force a child to face or overcome fears.

Age 4: At 4, children are stronger and more secure. A 4-year-old may boldly approach new challenges with an attitude of, "I'll try …" You can reinforce this courage to try new things like climbing to the top of the climbing gym or standing in front of the class to share a prized possession during "show and tell." But each 4-year-old is different and has different fears. In helping them manage fears, do what works best for each child. Go along with fantasy about monsters in the bathroom and shoo them out, then reinforce their understanding of reality by showing that there are no monsters in the bathroom or provide them with a special picture of Jesus to keep as a reminder of His protection. Tell or read stories about fearful situations to reassure 4-year-olds they are not alone in their fears or experiences.

Age 5: Most 5-year-olds venture into the world outside their families. They begin to recognize real dangers in life. They learn that people die, accidents happen, parents divorce, learning the alphabet is hard, and some kids are bullies. You can help them manage fears by acknowledging and validating the fear, and then helping them find a way to manage the fear and solve the problem. Managing a fear requires lots of small steps. Allow children at 5 to experience the process of managing fear. They can try avoiding the fearful situation, using pretend play to work through the fear, gaining information by reading about the fear, observing the fearful situation from a safe distance until feeling more comfortable, or by becoming comfortable through repeated small-dose exposure to the situation.

Teaching Activities

Keeping the Teaching Objective Alive in the Classroom: Tackling a Big Project

Materials Needed

- A large sheet of paper
- Masking tape
- Construction paper, assorted colors
- Scissors, adult- and child-sized
- Shoe box
- Glue sticks or glue, glue brushes and glue pots
- Pencil (optional)

What to Do

1. Tape a sheet of paper, large enough to prevent this project from being completed in a single day or by a single child but not so large that it is overwhelming, to the wall. Be sure to hang it low enough for children to reach it easily. Use separate pieces if you teach multiple classes.

2. Depending on the skill level and size of your class, two types of murals can be created. The first is a spontaneous and abstract mosaic with no planned pattern. The second, also a mosaic, involves creating a recognizable picture of the Bible story. If you choose the second option, sketch a simple drawing of David and Goliath on the paper.

3. Cut the construction paper into 1" strips. If your class will be creating a planned mosaic, separate the colors.

4. Set out the glue sticks or, if using white glue, pour the glue into the glue pots. (You might want to thin this glue with a little water.) Add the brushes.

5. Show the children how to cut the strips into 1" squares. Demonstrate how to glue the squares onto the mural paper. Emphasize the goal of completely covering the background. If your class will be creating the planned mosaic, show the children the appropriate place for each color. You might want to limit the work to a single color per day and devise a way to cover the areas that should not be filled in with the mosaic squares. Use plastic drop cloths or scrap paper to do this.

6. Whichever form of the mural you choose, continue the work on the mural daily until the entire sheet has been covered with bright squares of paper.

Teaching Bravery

- This project echoes the Bible story of a small child undertaking a large project. Draw this comparison for the children while encouraging them to retell the Bible story.

- Just as David did not face the giant alone, so the children will not face big projects alone. David had God and his slingshot. The children will have God, you, and each other. Reinforce that this project can be finished with God's help.

- Big and little, little and big. Reinforce this pair of opposites while working with the little squares on the big piece of paper.

Decorating the Bible Memory Verse: Crumpled Balls

Materials Needed

- Copies of the Bible memory verse (page 98), at least one per child
- Tissue paper, cut into big and little squares
- Glue
- Glue brushes
- Glue pots

What to Do

1. Set up for this art project as normal. Put the supplies on the art table. Pour the glue into the glue pots and add the brushes. You may want to thin the glue by adding a little water.

2. When the children arrive, demonstrate how to crumple a single square of tissue paper into a ball. Glue the balls onto the Bible memory verse.

Teaching Bravery

- Using big and little squares of tissue paper will produce large and small balls to reinforce this concept. Ask them to recall the big person, little person, and the use of the rocks in the story.

- Younger children might struggle with their fine motor control when making the crumpled balls. Praise them for their efforts, reminding them that trying a difficult task is a form of bravery. David fought the giant and won with God's

help. The children can crumple the balls with God's help. Lead them in a simple prayer to remind them of this.

- Be sure to read the Bible memory verse to the children. Help them recall the story by asking them who was afraid, who was brave, who had a shield, and who was David's shield.

Melt the Giant: A Circle-Time Game to Teach Bravery

Materials Needed

- Chalk
- Chalkboard (movable one works best)
- Plastic drop cloth or shower curtain
- 2–3 sponges
- Small bucket

What to Do

1. Draw a simple outline of the giant on the chalkboard. If you are using a movable chalkboard, you might want to roll it outside for this activity. If your chalkboard is stationary, place the drop cloth or shower curtain on the floor below it.

2. Fill the bucket with water. Dampen the sponges so they are wet, but not dripping.

3. During Circle Time, show the children how to throw the damp sponges at the giant. The water will cause the giant to disappear. Continue taking turns until the outline has vanished.

Teaching Bravery

- Encourage the children to support each other as they take turns throwing the sponges at the giant. This verbal support is in contrast to what David must have heard. Discuss this with the children. How do they feel when they hear encouraging remarks? How do they think David felt when he heard the dis-couraging remarks?

- Some of the children may hesitate to grab the wet sponge or put their hands into the water. Urge them to be brave, reminding them that God will be with them as they try new things. Most will overcome their hesitation. Praise them for this display of bravery.

- If the children have trouble hitting the giant, remind them to look him in the eye. Brave children can meet the eye of many people—and it will improve their accuracy too!

Blindly Brave: A Circle-Time Game to Teach Bravery

Materials Needed

- Pairs of stickers

- Blindfolds, enough for half of the children

- Chairs, tables, rope, broomsticks, blocks, etc.

What to Do

1. Use the props listed above to set up a simple obstacle course in your room. You might have a chair to walk around, a table to crawl under or over, a rope to walk on, a broomstick to jump over, or a path of blocks to navigate. Use your imagination and your resources to create a simple, safe course of 3–5 obstacles.

2. Hand out the stickers, one to each child. Tell them to place the stickers on their left hands, then find their partner, the child with the matching sticker. Have them sit down in pairs.

3. Demonstrate the obstacle course for the children. Show them when they must go around, under, over, or on top.

4. Hand out a blindfold to each pair of children. Have each child hold the blindfold over their face and discuss what it is like to be blindfolded.

5. Explain that one person in each pair will be blindfolded and one will be able to see. The sighted child will be responsible for leading the blindfolded child through the simple obstacle course. Allow the children to pick their roles, reminding them that they will switch in just a minute.

6. One pair at a time, blindfold a child and have one partner lead the other through the obstacle course. Reverse rolls and repeat.

Teaching Bravery

- Children need two things to be brave: preparation and faith. Help them prepare for this blind walk by discussing what it will be like to be blindfolded and by exploring the obstacle course. Discuss what it means to have faith in their partner or to be able to trust them. These small steps should make it possible for the children to accomplish this larger, scary goal.

- Are you willing to be led about blindfolded? Model your bravery by trying this daunting task yourself with another adult. Children learn best from examples.

- Praise attempts. Some children may not be able to do the whole obstacle course. Many may only handle one or two obstacles before becoming afraid. Praise their efforts. After all, David probably wrestled with his brothers and then fought wild animals before facing the giant. He, too, started small.

David and Goliath Puppets: A Craft Project to Teach the Story

Materials Needed

- Brown grocery bags, one per child
- Brown lunch bags, one per child
- Paper towel tubes, two per child
- Newspapers
- Duct tape
- Markers
- Buttons, four per child
- Yarn
- Scissors, adult-sized
- Glue

What to Do

1. Set up for this art project as you normally would. Cut the yarn into 8–10″ lengths.

2. Show the children how to crumple the newspapers and stuff both of their brown paper bags full. Insert a paper towel tube into each bag. Gather the opening of the bag and tape it to the tube using the duct tape. The large grocery bag is a Goliath puppet while the lunch bag is a David puppet. Explain the purpose of each bag to the children.

3. Glue the yarn on the top of the bags for hair and use buttons for eyes. Draw the remaining facial features with the markers.

Teaching Bravery

- Encourage the children to use the puppets to re-create the story, playing both the roles of David and Goliath. Gently correct any major mistakes in their stories.

- Help children distinguish between being loud and being brave. You might find them yelling loudly when they speak for the David puppet. Remind them a person can be quiet and still be brave.

- It is very important to praise their artistic attempts, assuring them that God is with them in their struggles.

From David to Goliath: A Center Activity to Teach the Story

Materials Needed

- From David to Goliath Reproducible pages (page 99–101)
- Poster board
- Scissors, adult-sized
- Marker
- 5 small baskets (berry baskets work well)

What to Do

1. Copy each of the From David to Goliath reproducible pages on the poster board.

2. Cut out each of the shapes. On the back of the smallest shape, use the marker to write "1"; on the back of the next smallest, write "2"; and so forth, numbering the largest figure in each set "5."

3. Sort the sets into separate baskets.

4. Introduce this independent center activity as normal. Demonstrate how to arrange the graduated sizes of the characters from smallest to largest. Encourage them to try it on their own.

5. Show the children how to self-check their work by looking at the numbers on the back of each figure. If arranged correctly, the numbers will be in order.

Teaching Bravery

- As the children arrange the figures, help them retell the story of David and Goliath.

- Who was smaller, David or Goliath? (David) Remind the children that he was able to overcome the giant with God's help. How has God helped them to be brave? How has He been their shield? Share an example from your own life, remembering that courage is best taught by example.

Take Aim: A Circle-Time Game to Teach the Memory Verse

Materials Needed

- Take Aim Reproducible pages (page 102–104)
- Poster board, 5 pieces
- Masking tape
- Copy of the Bible memory verse (page 98)
- 5 beanbags

What to Do

1. Copy the reproducible pages onto the poster board. Tape them to the ground in a line in front of the children.

2. Read the Bible memory verse with the children several times. Encourage them to repeat it with you.

3. Show the class the pictures that illustrate the verse. Give the first child the beanbags. Have her toss the beanbags one at a time, in order, onto the Rebus pictures. Help her say the corresponding words of the Bible memory verse out loud, including the reference.

4. Repeat, allowing each child a chance.

Teaching Bravery

- This game builds on the previous five units in this book. Thank the children who are waiting patiently; compliment them for acting like Abraham and Sarah. Admire those children who use kind words; praise them for acting like Ruth. Acknowledge those children who share willingly; thank them for acting like good friends David and Jonathan. Is there a mishap? Help those involved to ask for and grant forgiveness; point them to Mary as their model. Are the children saying please and thank you? If so, commend them for acting like the thankful leper. If most of the children are exhibiting a majority of these behaviors, congratulate yourself on being brave enough to undertake teaching God's little lambs.

- Do you remember the two basic elements of courage? Preparation and faith? Encourage the children to practice tossing the beanbags and to have faith that they can hit the targets. Then praise them for being brave in their attempts.

- Is this a new skill for some of the children? Remind them that trying something new is another way of demonstrating courage.

- Remember to look the children in the eye as you praise them. Eye contact models another way of showing courage.

David's Shield: A Craft Project to Teach the Bible Memory Verse

Materials Needed

- Corrugated cardboard, one piece per child
- Pencil
- Scissors, adult- and child-sized
- Duct tape
- Shield Bible memory verse (page 105), one copy per child
- Glue sticks

- Glitter
- Funnel
- 3–4 Styrofoam trays

What to Do

1. Draw a simple shield shape on the cardboard, making one for each child. Each shield should be about 10″ × 12″.

2. Cut out each shield.

3. For each shield, cut two pieces of duct tape, one about 5″ long and the other about 3″ long. Center the shorter piece of tape on the longer one, sticky side to sticky side. Press together firmly. Use the extended sticky sides to tape this handle onto the back of each shield.

4. Put the shields, scissors, copies of the Shield Bible memory verse, glue sticks, glitter, funnel, and Styrofoam trays on the art table.

5. When the children arrive, show them how to cut out the Shield Bible memory verse on the solid line. Let them glue it onto the front of their shield.

6. Show them how to put glue across the front of the shield. Sprinkle the glitter on top of the glue. Shake the excess glitter onto a Styrofoam tray.

7. Using the funnel, pour the glitter from the Styrofoam tray back into the glitter container.

Teaching Bravery

- Read the Bible memory verse individually with the children. Ask them what they think it means to have the Lord as their shield. Accept any reasonable answer, guiding them toward a clearer understanding of the phrase when necessary.

- Ask the children some questions about the story: Who had a shield? (King Saul)

Who did not? (David) Who was afraid? (King Saul and the well-armed Israelites) Who was not? (David and his five smooth stones) Who was really David's shield? (The Lord) Who is our shield, even when we do not have this toy shield with us? (The Lord)

- Encourage the children to play with the shield. Help them speculate how it kept a warrior safe. Compare this shield to the Lord's protection. Fantasy play offers children opportunities to master their fears. Use your imagination to help the children overcome their fears through fantasy play.

- Ask each child to stand up, hold their shield, and recite the Bible memory verse.

Telling the Story

To tell the story for this unit, first review the story by reading 1 Samuel 17:4–54. Then gather the following supplies to make puppets for the story: large garbage bag (kitchen trash can size or larger), small plastic bag (wastepaper bag, 4-gallon size), two wrapping paper tubes, newspapers, duct tape, construction paper, and scissors. Crumple the newspaper and stuff both plastic bags until they are almost full. Insert a wrapping paper tube into each bag. Gather the opening of the bag and tape it to the tube using the duct tape. (See diagram.)

Cut out facial features from the construction paper and tape them onto the bags. Five stones (balls of crumpled paper), a slingshot, a shepherd's bag, a sword, and helmet are props that make this ancient story come alive. Read the following story written in bold print while you follow the directions given in italics.

Who knows what a giant is? *Pause for answers.* **Are giants real or pretend?** *Pause for answers.* **A long time ago, long before you**

duct tape

wrapping paper tube

were born, before your grandfather was born, before Jesus was born, there lived a giant named Goliath. At the same time, there lived a young boy named David, who was a shepherd. Does anyone remember David from another story? *The children should remember David from the unit on friendship or they may remember him from a Sunday school lesson.* Now, even though we do not see giants today, we know that David really met the giant Goliath because it is written in the Bible and everything written in God's Word is the truth. *Select three children to help you act out this story. Let one hold the large Goliath puppet; the second holds the smaller David puppet; and the third holds the sword and helmet. All of the other children can either watch the two puppeteers or pretend to be soldiers.*

Now the Philistines—those are the bad guys—were fighting the Israelites. The Philistines camped on one hill and the Israelites on another, with the valley between them. Every day, a soldier named Goliath came out of the Philistine camp. *Motion for Goliath to come out and raise his puppet high in the air. Tell the puppeteer to pantomime Goliath's actions.* He was over nine feet tall. Goliath would stand and shout to the Israelites, "Come out and fight me! Are you afraid? Choose a brave man and have

him come to fight me! If he is able to kill me, then you will win the war. But if I kill him, you will become our slaves. Surely there is one brave man who will fight me!"

King Saul and all the Israelites looked at Goliath. Every soldier was too scared to fight the giant. Day after day, Goliath came out and teased the Israelites. The Israelites tried to pretend that he wasn't there. *Tell the soldiers not to look at the giant.*

Now David had three older brothers who were fighting with Saul—and like all the other soldiers, they were also scared of Goliath. One day, David's father gave David some food and told him to take it to his older brothers. So, early the next morning, David went to the Israelite's camp. *Motion for the David puppet to come and stand opposite the Goliath puppet.* He quickly found his brothers and gave them the food. Then he watched as Goliath came out and began to yell his taunts at the Israelites. *Pantomime the taunting and pacing.* David was sad when he realized that his brothers and all the other soldiers were too scared to fight the giant.

David said to King Saul, "I will go and fight the giant. I am not afraid of him because the Lord will help me." *Have David say this to you.*

Saul replied, "You cannot fight him; you are only a boy, and he has been a soldier for many years."

But David said to Saul, "I have killed both the lion and the bear. I can fight this giant."

So Saul said to David, "Go, and the Lord be with you. But please, wear my armor and helmet so that you will be well protected. Take my sword and shield too." *Tell the child to give the helmet and sword to the David puppeteer.*

David put on King Saul's armor and helmet. Then he put on the sword and tried walking around. *Help the puppet try to manage King Saul's gear.* "I cannot use these," he said to Saul. "They are too big for me!" So he took them off. Then David chose five smooth stones, put them in the pouch of his shepherd's bag, and, with his sling in his hand, approached the giant. *Hand the puppeteer the appropriate props.*

When David reached Goliath, the giant saw that he was only a boy. Goliath said, "You are too little to fight me! You should be scared of me, you little boy! Go away and send a real man out to fight me."

David answered, "You come against me with sword and spear, but I come against you in the name of the Lord Almighty, the God of the armies of Israel. This day the Lord will hand you over to me so I am not afraid. When I win, all of the soldiers will know that it is not by sword or spear that the Lord saves. The battle is the Lord's, and He will help me win. The Lord will make me brave. The Lord will be my shield."

David ran quickly toward the giant. Reaching into his bag and taking out a stone, he threw it from his sling, and the stone hit Goliath on the forehead. *Tell David to act this out. Wait for success.* The giant fell face down on the ground. *Have Goliath lie down.* David won—the brave boy fought the giant and won with the Lord's help.

Repeat this story if there are others who would like to be puppeteers or other actors.

Bible Memory Verse

The LORD is my strength and my shield.

Psalm 28:7 (NIV)

From David to Goliath, page 1

 David

 Soldier

David's Brother

King Saul

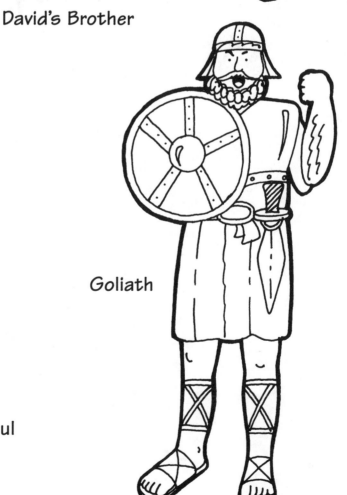 Goliath

From David to Goliath, page 2

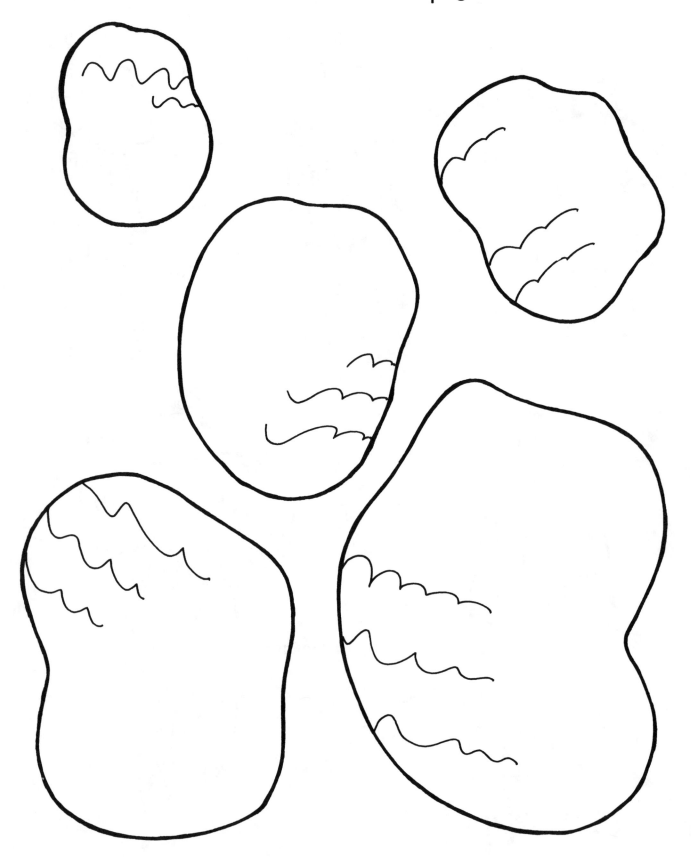

From David to Goliath, page 3

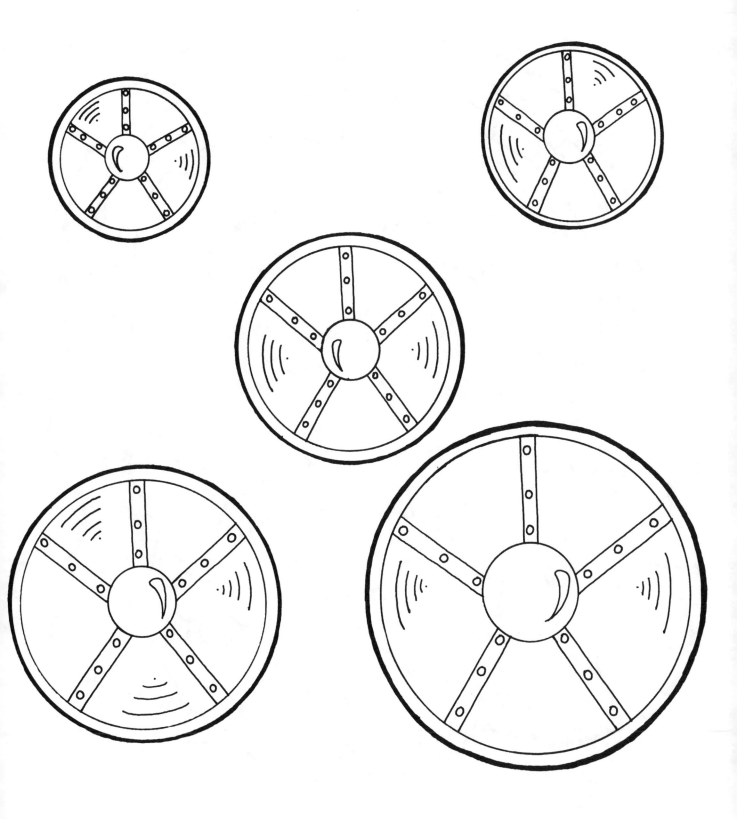

Take Aim, page 1

Take Aim, page 1

Take Aim, page 2

Take Aim, page 3

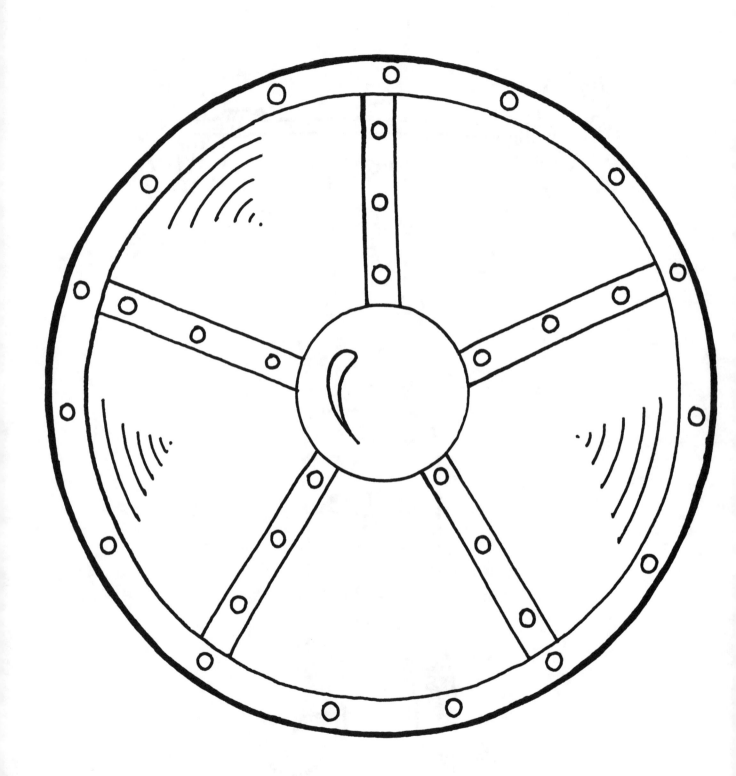

Shield Bible Memory Verse

The Lord is my strength and my shield.

Psalm 28:7 (NIV)

The Lord is my strength and my shield.

Psalm 28:7 (NIV)

Dear Parent(s),

"Please be brave!" It's difficult for your child to be brave in the dark, when having a scraped knee bandaged, when getting an immunization, when going off alone to preschool. David was brave when he faced the enemy giant Goliath. This month our class will learn how David trusted God and overcame his fear.

The lessons of David and courage should not stop at the classroom door. I invite you to share these lessons with your child at home by reading the story of David and Goliath from a preschool Bible, trying the activities provided in this letter, and teaching this Bible memory verse.

The LORD is my strength and my shield. *Psalm 28:7*

How Children Learn to Have Courage

Age 3: Fear of the dark, fear of monsters, fear of new situations, fear of animals—3-year-olds are beginning to develop rich fantasy lives and are starting to realize the world can be a dangerous and scary place. At 3, a child needs to have those fears accepted and respected. Time is needed to adjust to scary situations. Your child's trust will grow as you keep promises, provide protection, encourage trying new things, and generously praise efforts. This is a good time to protect your child from fears, allow room to express fears, and be present to provide support in frightening situations. It is not a good idea to force a child to face or overcome fears.

Age 4: At 4, children are stronger and more secure. A 4-year-old may boldly approach new challenges with an attitude of, "I'll try …" You can reinforce this courage to try new things like climbing to the top of the climbing gym or standing in front of the class to share a prized possession during "show and tell." But each 4-year-old is different and has different fears. In helping them manage fears, do what works best for each child. Go along with fantasy about monsters in the bathroom and shoo them out, then reinforce their understanding of reality by showing that there are no monsters in the bathroom or provide them with a special picture of Jesus to keep as a reminder of His protection. Tell or read stories about fearful situations to reassure 4-year-olds they are not alone in their fears or experiences.

Age 5: Most 5-year-olds venture into the world outside their families. They begin to recognize real dangers in life. They learn that people die, accidents happen, parents divorce, learning the alphabet is hard, and some kids are bullies. You can help them manage fears by acknowledging and validating the fear, and then helping them find a way to manage the fear and solve the problem. Managing a fear requires lots of small steps. Allow children at 5 to experience the process of managing fear. They can try avoiding the fearful situation, using pretend play to work through the fear, gaining information by reading about the fear, observing the fearful situation from a safe distance until feeling more comfortable, or by becoming comfortable through repeated small-dose exposure to the situation.

Parent's Prayer

Heavenly Father, I want my child to trust me for protection and care, yet I often fail to trust in You. David's faith gave him the courage to stand up to a giant problem. Lord, give me the courage to trust in You as I face life's problems. Help me to show faith and courage so that my child will also learn to stand up to fears and trust in Your protective arms. In Jesus' name I pray. Amen.

Together in Christ,

Family Activities

Peanut Butter Rocks: A Cooking Adventure

Ingredients

- 1 cup peanut butter
- 3 tablespoons honey
- 1 cup nonfat dry milk powder
- Chopped nuts, crunchy cereal, or mini-chocolate chips
- Measuring cups
- Measuring spoons
- Large bowl
- Wooden spoon
- Small bowl
- Wax paper

What to Do

1. Help your child measure the ingredients into the large bowl. Use the wooden spoon to mix well, adding more nonfat dry milk powder if the dough is still very sticky. You might have to use your hands to thoroughly mix the ingredients.

2. Pour the chopped nuts, crunchy cereal, or mini-chocolate chips into the small bowl.

3. Pinch off small amounts of the peanut butter dough and roll into balls. Demonstrate this rolling technique to your child.

4. Help your child roll the peanut butter balls in the chopped nuts, crunchy cereal, or mini-chocolate chips. Place on wax paper.

5. Eat!

Teaching Bravery

- Many young children hesitate at getting their hands into this sticky mix. Reassure your child that this fear is normal and acceptable and to try touching the dough. If still unwilling to touch or mix the dough, praise the effort. It takes courage to try something new!

- Some preschoolers will struggle with the task of rolling dough balls. Praise your child's bravery for attempting to learn a new skill. Talk about God being with us as we learn.

- Help your child remember the story by asking the following questions: Whom were the Israelites afraid of? (Goliath, the giant) Who was not afraid of him? (David) What did David use to fight Goliath? (Smooth stones and a slingshot) How many stones did he take with him? (Five) Can you count five stones? (Help your child count five peanut butter rocks.)

Stone Art: An Art Project

Materials Needed

- Large, flat rock (porous rocks such as sandstone work best)
- Washable tempera paint, one color
- Styrofoam tray
- Variety of items to use as brushes: string, balls, plastic dolls, plastic knife, cardboard, toy pieces, etc.
- Traditional brushes
- Newspapers
- Smock for your child

What to Do

1. Assemble all the needed supplies. If you are unable to find a suitable rock, you can try this project on paper.

2. Cover the work surface with newspapers. Pour the paint into the Styrofoam tray. Place the smock on your child.

3. Dip any of the items into the paint and use them to paint on the rock.

4. Experiment with designs, patterns, or pictures.

5. Let dry completely.

Teaching Bravery

- As you and your child paint, speculate how David, Goliath, and King Saul felt during this battle. The Bible says Saul was frightened while David was courageous. Perhaps your child has a fear of something. Choose an object to represent this fear and paint on the stone with it. Talk about this fear in a non-threatening manner. Help your child list some solutions for overcoming this fear. Offer congratulations for being brave enough to face this fear.

- Use the different items used as brushes to help your child recall the story. Ask the following questions: String—Who used a slingshot? (David) Balls—What did he put in the slingshot? (Smooth stones) Plastic dolls—Who fought whom? (Goliath and David fought with each other.) Plastic knife—What weapon did Saul offer David? (A sword) Ask any other questions that the different brushes inspire.

David's Harp: A Craft Project

Materials Needed

- Empty tissue box
- 3–5 rubber bands of varying thicknesses
- Markers, crayons, paint, etc.

What to Do

1. Assemble all the needed materials. If so inspired, decorate the empty tissue box with markers, crayons, and paint.
2. Put the rubber bands around the empty tissue box so they stretch across the opening.
3. Pluck the harp's strings. Sing a verse from a psalm. (Psalm 27 is a good choice.) Make up your own melody.

Teaching Bravery

- Courage is made up of two parts: preparation and faith. Help your child prepare to sing the song and then have the faith to try the tune. These simple steps should raise the comfort level with this new experience.
- Be sure to model bravery by singing your own simple melody and words out loud. Children learn best from what they see, not from what they are told.
- Ask your child the following questions about the story: What did David take to his brothers? (Food) How do you think the Israelites felt when Goliath was killed? (Happy, excited, not afraid anymore) What kind of songs might the winning army have sung? (Make one up—see Psalm 18 for ideas.)

Other Simple Ideas

1. Toss rocks at a target, but tell your child never to use a sibling or other person as the target.
2. Practice looking each other in the eye as you talk. Courageous people can make good eye contact.